# えいごで日記 文法

### Let's write a diary in English!

## 動詞・時制

能島 久美江

アルゴクラブ in English 主宰

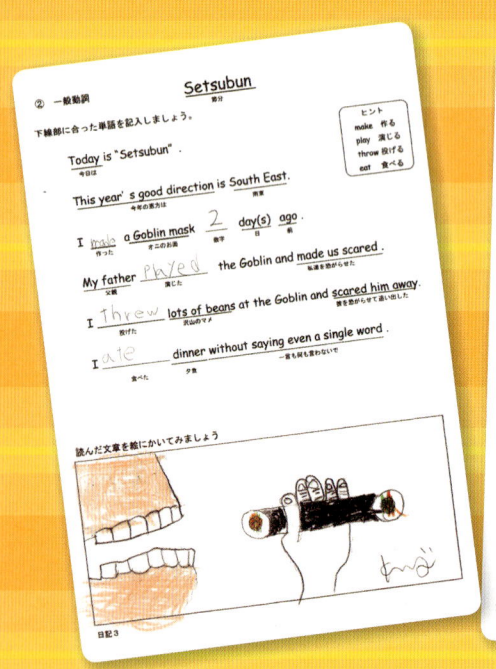

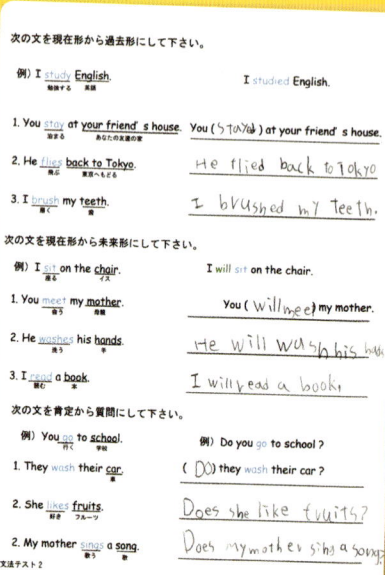

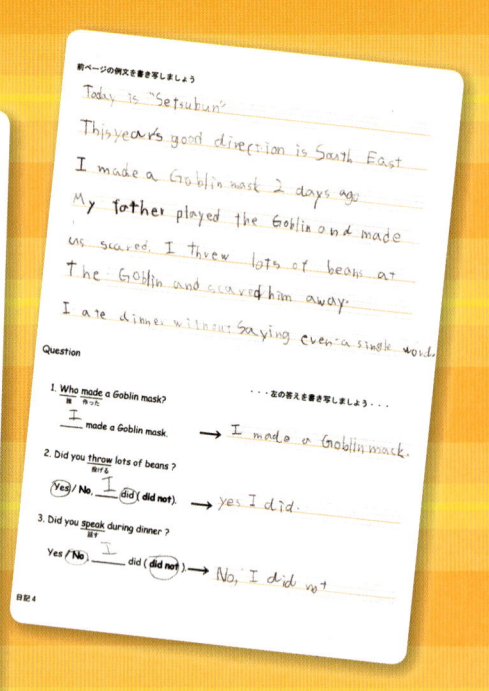

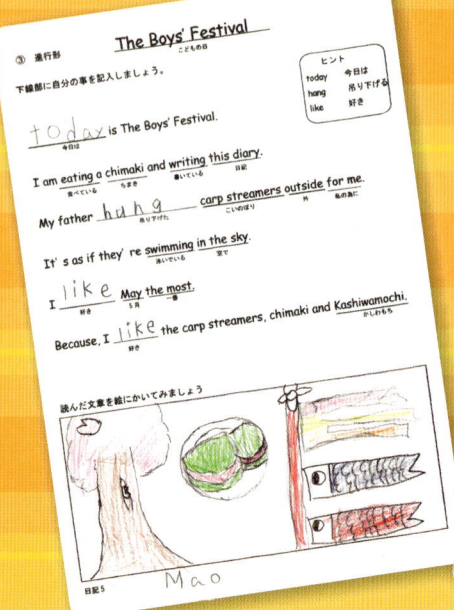

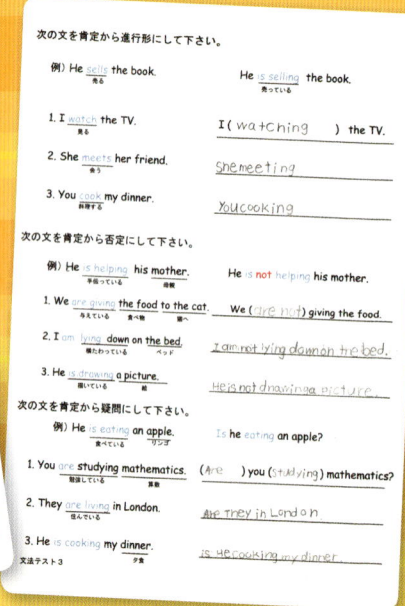

※子ども英語教室「アルゴクラブ in English」にて、9歳の子どもたちが実際に書いた「えいご日記」です

# えいごで日記 文法 動詞/時制

## はじめに

### 保護者の方へ

　私の教室では、本書の「時制チャート」と「日記シート」を使用して、小学生から「英語の時制を英語で」教えています。

　もちろん、まだ英語力がつたない子どもたちなので、レッスン前に日本語で簡単な説明をします。その後はすべて英語だけでの取り組みですが、それらがスムーズに実現しています。

　いったん自分の頭の中で理解できれば、後は単語をたくさん覚えればいいだけです。生徒たちを見て「英文法を使いこなすのは、なんら難しいことではない」と確信し、日々のレッスンや息子たちとの試行錯誤の中から作り上げたのが本書です。

　私のレッスンでは、「まず英文の仕組みを図（チャート）でイメージさせる」ことを重視しています。
　子どもたちは、それぞれ自分で理解します。もし途中でわからなくなっても、またチャートを見るとすぐ思い出し、自分たちで英文を作成していくことができます。この繰り返し作業で英語の時制、つまり英文法を習得していきます。
　日本では、「子どもたちに文法を説明しても、理解して活用できるようになるのは難しいのでは…」と思われがちです。しかし世界では、母語が英語でない小学生が、授業で当たり前のように英文法を習い、使いこなしています。
　「文法を英語で身につける」ことは、とても自然な英語習得の近道なのです。

　自分の能力を表現するためのツール（英語）を持つだけで、世界中に自分をアピールできるようになります。世界のどこへ行っても仕事ができ、勉強ができるのです。
　私は将来、日本の子どもたちが英語をツールとして自分たちの能力を使い、世界の舞台で活躍してくれることを楽しみにしています。

能島 久美江

※本書のチャートとシートは、2006年12月に実用新案登録を認可されました。（登録第3128500号）

# Contents   もくじ

| | |
|---|---|
| はじめに | 3 |
| 『えいごで日記 文法 動詞・時制』の使い方 | 6 |
| 主語の活用法 | 9 |
| 時制の一覧表　1 | 10 |

**Part 1　be動詞 Be Verb**　11
Practice 練習 … 14　　Practice Test 確認テスト … 15
Diary えいご日記 … 16

**Part 2　一般動詞 Simple Verb**　19
Practice 練習 … 22　　Practice Test 確認テスト … 29
Diary えいご日記 … 30

**Part 3　進行形 Continuous**　33
Practice 練習 … 36　　Practice Test 確認テスト … 37
Diary えいご日記 … 38

**Part 4　受動態 Passive**　41
Practice 練習 … 44　　Practice Test 確認テスト … 45
Diary えいご日記 … 46

| Part 5 | 受動態 進行形 Passive Continuous<br>Practice 練習 … 52　Practice Test 確認テスト … 53<br>Diary えいご日記 … 54 | 49 |

| 解答 1 | 57 |

| 時制の一覧表 2 | 58 |

| Part 6 | 完了形 Perfect<br>Practice 練習 … 62　Practice Test 確認テスト … 63<br>Diary えいご日記 … 64 | 59 |

| Part 7 | 完了形 進行形 Perfect Continuous<br>Practice 練習 … 70　Practice Test 確認テスト … 71<br>Diary えいご日記 … 72 | 67 |

| Part 8 | 完了形 受動態 Perfect Passive<br>Practice 練習 … 78　Practice Test 確認テスト … 79<br>Diary えいご日記 … 80 | 75 |

| Part 9 | Can 重要な助動詞<br>Practice 練習 … 86　Practice Test 確認テスト … 87<br>Diary えいご日記 … 88 | 83 |

| 解答 2 | 91 |

| ふろく（規則動詞の変化表／不規則動詞の変化表） | 92 |

five 5

## ●『えいごで日記 文法 動詞・時制』の使い方 ●

### イメージ作業から「時制チャート」へ

　本書は、「動詞の変化」を重視して作成しています。なぜなら英語では、動詞の変化によってさまざまな「時の流れ」を表すからです。「動詞の変化のしかた」をマスターすれば、いろいろな「時の流れ」を表現できるようになります。

　「時の流れ」と「動詞の変化」の関係については、「自分の体」を使ってイメージするのが効果的です。

1. 頭が「現在（肯定）」、胸が「現在（否定）」、腰が「現在（疑問）」。
2. 左肩が「過去（肯定）」、左手が「過去（否定）」、左足が「過去（疑問）」。
3. 右肩が「未来（肯定）」、右手が「未来（否定）」、右足が「未来（疑問）」。

これで、それぞれの「時の流れ」が体の一部で常にイメージできますね！

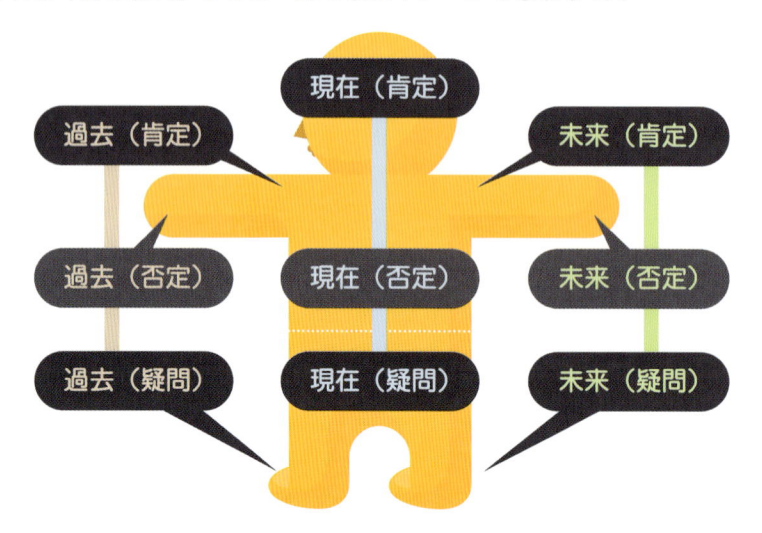

このイメージ作業は、以下の「時制チャート」を見ながら行ってくださいね。

|  | 過去 | 現在 | 未来 |
|---|---|---|---|
| ○ 肯定 | 左肩 | 頭 | 右肩 |
| × 否定 | 左手 | 胸 | 右手 |
| ? 疑問 | 左足 | 腰 | 右足 |

　「時制チャート」はそれぞれの動詞ごとに、左から時の流れに沿って **"過去 - 現在 - 未来"** となり、上段から下段に向かって **"肯定形 - 否定形 - 疑問形"** となっています。

　この「時制チャート」をイメージで頭に入れておくと、動詞の変化を簡単に覚え、活用できるようになります。

『えいごで日記 文法 動詞・時制』の使い方

## 「時制チャート」から「日記シート」へ

左ページのように、「時制チャート」を用いて「時の流れ」と「動詞の変化」の関係が理解できたら、次は「日記シート」を使って、英文を書き始めてみましょう。
以下が「日記シート」の使い方です。

① 自分の書きたい主語を選ぶ

② 動詞を選ぶ。（時制チャートを思い浮かべながら、「時の流れ」に注意して選ぼう）
※文字の色も参考にしてね。

③ 選んだ語句を書き出してつなげる。

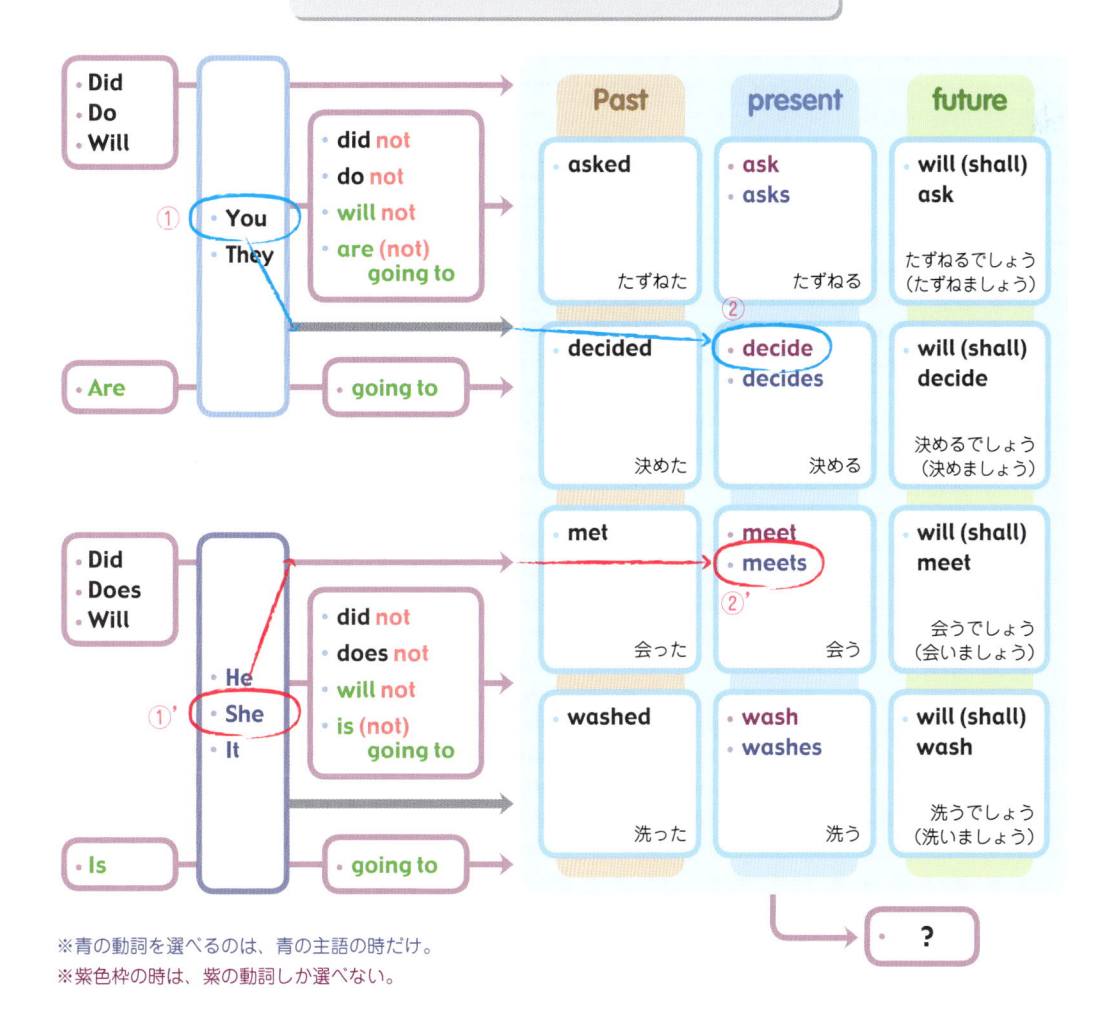

| 主語グループ | 助動詞 | 否定形 | Past | present | future |
|---|---|---|---|---|---|
| • Did / • Do / • Will | ① • You / • They | • did not / • do not / • will not / • are (not) going to | • asked (たずねた) | • ask / • asks (たずねる) | • will (shall) ask (たずねるでしょう／たずねましょう) |
| • Are | | • going to | • decided (決めた) | ② • decide / • decides (決める) | • will (shall) decide (決めるでしょう／決めましょう) |
| • Did / • Does / • Will | ①' • He / • She / • It | • did not / • does not / • will not / • is (not) going to | • met (会った) | • meet / ②' • meets (会う) | • will (shall) meet (会うでしょう／会いましょう) |
| • Is | | • going to | • washed (洗った) | • wash / • washes (洗う) | • will (shall) wash (洗うでしょう／洗いましょう) |
| | | | | • ? | |

※青の動詞を選べるのは、青の主語の時だけ。
※紫色枠の時は、紫の動詞しか選べない。

③の例）　**You decide ...**　あなたは決める…
　　　　　**She meets ...**　彼女は会う…

動詞の後ろの要素は、表現したい内容に応じて追加しよう。

文の最後には「.」を付けるのを忘れないでね。
※最後が「？」の時は不要

## ● 『えいごで日記 文法 動詞・時制』の使い方 ●

イメージ作業ができたら、
実際に文章を作成してみよう！

**Practice / 練習**

英文作成の練習に挑戦。
その次は、主語をいろいろ置き換えて、自分で英文を作成してください。

簡単にマスターできましたよね！

時制が理解できているか、
確認のテストをしてみよう！

**Practice Test / 確認テスト**

確認テストに挑戦！

例があるから１人でもできる！

えいご日記に挑戦！

**Diary / えいご日記**

1. 日本語のヒントを見ながら、下線部に当てはまる語句を入れてください。
2. 日記の文章を絵に描いてください。
　（文章をイメージとして頭に入れる練習です）
3. 完成させた文章を、すべて最初から書き写してください。
　（これは、英文を書く練習ですね）
4. **Question** に挑戦してね。

日記で見ると時間の流れがよくわかるね

自分で文章を作ってみよう！

この一連の作業を、すべての Part で繰り返し行ってください。
１冊を終了する頃には、英文法の大きな幹が体の中にできているはずです。
その大きな幹にどのような葉・花をつけるかは、もちろん単語力やその他、前置詞の使い方・修飾語・副詞…などなどたくさんの要素で変わってきます。
しかし、しっかりとした幹でなくては、美しい花を咲かせることはできません。
英文法は英語でイメージしながら学べば簡単で、あっという間に理解でき、使いこなせるようになることを実感してください。

## 主語の活用表

本書では、主語などの使い方を詳しく説明していませんので、
下記の一覧表を参考にしてください。

| | ～は／～が | | ～の | | ～に・を | ～のもの |
|---|---|---|---|---|---|---|
| 私 | I | am | my | book 本 / cat 猫 | me | mine |
| あなた（たち） | You | are | your | dog 犬 / car 車 / pen ペン / bird 鳥 | you | yours |
| 私たち | We | | our | | us | ours |
| 彼ら・彼女ら・それら | They | | their | | them | theirs |
| 彼 | He | is | his | bag カバン / cup カップ / watch 時計 / pet ペット | him | his |
| 彼女 | She | | her | | her | hers |
| それ | It | | its | | it | its |

### 物が1つの時

| | | |
|---|---|---|
| これは | This | is |
| あれは | That | |
| あります | There | |

### 物が2つ以上の時

| | | |
|---|---|---|
| これらは | These | are |
| あれらは | Those | |
| あります | There | |

# 時制の一覧表 1

※ do は動詞の原形、did は過去形、done は過去分詞形を表す。

| | Past 過去 | Present 現在 | Future 未来 |
|---|---|---|---|
| **part 1** Be 動詞 Be Verb p.11 | was / were 〜でした | is / am / are 〜です | is・am・are + going to be / will + be 〜でしょう |
| **part 2** 一般動詞 Simple Verb p.19 | did 〜しました | do + s/es 〜します | will / shall + do 〜するでしょう / 〜しましょう |
| **part 3** 進行形 Continuous p.33 | was・were + do + ing 〜していた | is・am・are + do + ing 〜しています | will / shall + be + do+ing 〜しているでしょう |
| **part 4** 受動態 Passive p.41 | was・were + done 〜された | is・am・are + done 〜される | will / shall + be + done 〜されるでしょう |
| **part 5** 受動態進行形 Passive Continuous p.49 | was・were + being +done 〜され続けていた | is・am・are + being +done 〜され続けている | will / shall +be+ being+done 〜され続けているでしょう ※文法上は可能だが、実生活においてはあまり使用されない。 |

# Part 1

# be動詞

Be Verb

主語（私は・あなたは… など）を
「〜です」と表現する時に使う動詞です。

## Part 1 — Be Verb

# ● be動詞

### 主語 ＋ be 動詞

|  | **Past** 過去 | **Present** 現在 | **Future** 未来<br>・will do<br>・going to do（すでに計画している） |
|---|---|---|---|
| **○ Positive 肯定** | ・I was<br>・You / We / They were<br>・He / She / It was<br><br>〜でした | ・I am<br>・You / We / They are<br>・He / She / It is<br><br>〜です | ・I am<br>・You / We / They are<br>・He / She / It is<br>　└ going to be<br>・I / You/We/They / He/She/It　will be<br><br>〜でしょう |
| **✕ Negative 否定** | ・I was<br>・You / We / They were<br>・He / She / It was<br>　└ not<br>〜ではありませんでした | ・I am<br>・You / We / They are<br>・He / She / It is<br>　└ not<br>〜ではありません | ・I am<br>・You / We / They are<br>・He / She / It is<br>　└ not　└ going to be<br>・I / You/We/They / He/ She / It　will not be<br>〜ではないでしょう |
| **? Question 疑問** | ・Was I<br>・Were you / we / they …?<br>・Was he / she / it …?<br><br>〜でしたか？ | ・Am I …?<br>・Are you / we / they …?<br>・Is he / she / it …?<br><br>〜ですか？ | ・Am I<br>・Are you / we / they<br>・Is he / she / it<br>　└ going to be …?<br>・Will　I / you/we/they / he/ she / it　be …?<br>〜でしょうか？ |

過去　　　現在　　　未来

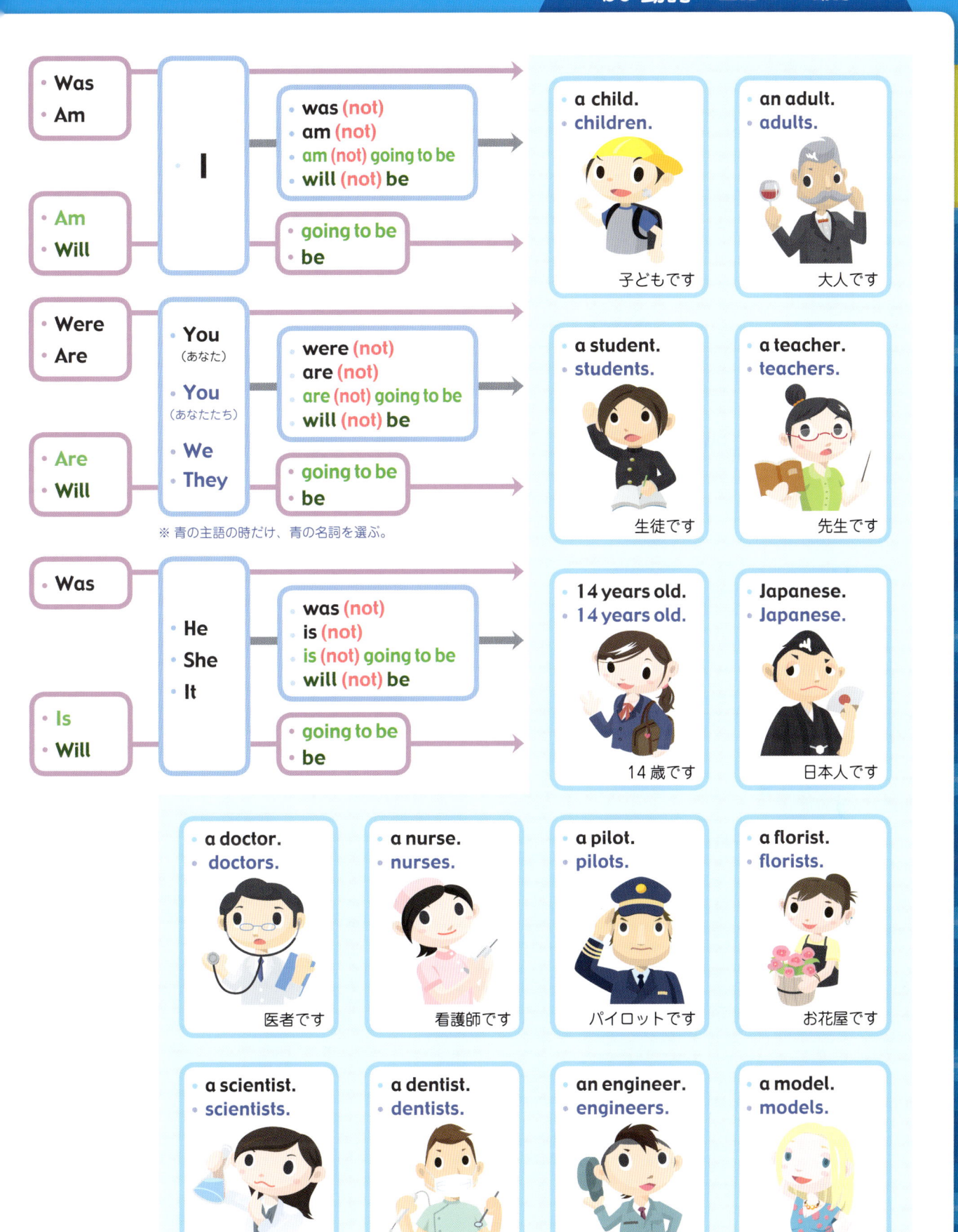

## be 動詞　主語 + be 動詞

**Part 1**

- Was
- Am

→ I →
- was (not)
- am (not)
- am (not) going to be
- will (not) be

→
- a child. / children. （子どもです）
- an adult. / adults. （大人です）

- Am
- Will

→ I →
- going to be
- be

- Were
- Are

→ You (あなた) / You (あなたたち) / We / They →
- were (not)
- are (not)
- are (not) going to be
- will (not) be

→
- a student. / students. （生徒です）
- a teacher. / teachers. （先生です）

- Are
- Will

→
- going to be
- be

※ 青の主語の時だけ、青の名詞を選ぶ。

- Was

→ He / She / It →
- was (not)
- is (not)
- is (not) going to be
- will (not) be

→
- 14 years old. / 14 years old. （14歳です）
- Japanese. / Japanese. （日本人です）

- Is
- Will

→
- going to be
- be

- a doctor. / doctors. （医者です）
- a nurse. / nurses. （看護師です）
- a pilot. / pilots. （パイロットです）
- a florist. / florists. （お花屋です）
- a scientist. / scientists. （科学者です）
- a dentist. / dentists. （歯医者です）
- an engineer. / engineers. （エンジニアです）
- a model. / models. （モデルです）

※ 紫色枠の時は、最後の「.」を取る。 → ?

thirteen 13

## Be Verb

Part 1

### Practice / 練習

● P.12～13を参考に、自分で文章を作成してみよう。

**現在形**

I am _____ .

I am not _____ .

**過去形**

I was _____ .

I was not _____ .

**未来形**

I am going to be _____ .

I am not going to be _____ .

**疑問形**

Are you _____ ?

Were you _____ ?

Are you going to be _____ ?

# Practice Test / 確認テスト

**be 動詞　主語 + be動詞**

**Part 1**

① 次の文を現在形から過去形にしてみよう。　　　　　　　　　　　　　　　　※解答は P.57

例）She *is* a cabin attendant.　☞　She *was* a cabin attendant.
　　　　　キャビンアテンダント

1. I *am* a student.　　　　　　　☞　I _____ a student.
　　　　　生徒

2. You *are* young.　　　　　　　☞　_____
　　　　　　若い

3. He *is* from Tokyo.　　　　　　☞　_____
　　　　　　東京出身

② 次の文を現在形から未来形にしてみよう。

例）He *is* a soccer player.　☞　He *is going to be* a soccer player.
　　　　　サッカー選手

1. I *am* a doctor.　　　　　　　☞　I _____ a doctor.
　　　　　医者

2. They *are* 12 years old.　　　☞　_____
　　　　　　　12歳

3. She *is* my friend.　　　　　　☞　_____
　　　　　　　友達

③ 次の文を肯定から否定にしてみよう。

例）You *are* an American.　☞　You *are not* an American.
　　　　　アメリカ人

1. They *are* friends.　　　　　　☞　They _____ friends.

2. She *is* my older sister.　　　☞　_____
　　　　　　　年上の　姉妹

3. I *am* young.　　　　　　　　　☞　_____

## Be Verb

Part 1

**Diary / えいご日記**

**The New School Year**
新学期

● 下線部に自分のことを記入して、えいご日記を完成させよう。

The new school year starts today.
　　　　　　　　　　　　開始　　今日

I am in class _____ . My teacher's name is _____ .
　　　　　組　（自分のクラス名）　　私の先生の名前　　　　（自分の先生の名前）

The person sitting next to me is called _____ .
　　隣の席の人　　　　　　　　　　　呼ばれる　（その人の名前）

_____ is a student. _____ is _____ years old.
彼／彼女　　生徒　　　彼／彼女　（年齢の数字）　〜歳

There are _____ boys in the class.
　　　　（人数）　男の子たち

There are _____ girls in the class.
　　　　（人数）　女の子たち

My new class is very fun!
　　新しいクラス　　とても楽しい

● 上の文章を絵に描いてみよう。

be 動詞　主語 ＋ be 動詞

Part 1

● 左ページの日記を書き写そう。

## Question

● 質問に答えよう。その答えを下に書き写そう。

1. *Is your teacher an <u>adult</u>?*
   　　　　　　　　　　　　大人

   ☞　Yes, [ ・he / ・she ] is. / No, [ ・he / ・she ] is not.　　※左から答えを選んでね。

2. *<u>How old</u> is the person sitting next to you?*
   　　いくつ

   ☞　_____ is _____ years old.
   　　He / She

※本書では、子どもたちに単語の1つ1つを理解させるために、"isn't" のような縮約形は使用していません。

seventeen 17

## Be Verb

Part 1

● 文章を自分で作ってみよう。

● 文章を自分で作ってみよう。

# Part 2

# 一般動詞
## Simple Verb

主語（私は・あなたは… など）が、
「〜する」と 動作を表現する時に使う動詞です。

## Simple Verb

# 一般動詞

**主語 ＋ 動詞**

Part 2

### Past 過去

**Positive 肯定**
- I
- You / We / They
- He / She / It
  - did

〜しました

**Negative 否定**
- I
- You / We / They
- He / She / It
  - did not do

〜しませんでした

**Question 疑問**
- Did
  - I do …?
  - you / we / they do …?
  - he / she / it do …?

〜しましたか？

### Present 現在

**Positive**
- I do
- You / We / They do
- He / She / It does

〜します

**Negative**
- I do
- You / We / They do
- He / She / It does
  - not do

〜しません

**Question**
- Do
  - I do …?
  - you / we / they do …?
- Does
  - he / she / it do …?

〜しますか？

### Future 未来
- will do
- shall do (提案する / 誘う)
- going to do (すでに計画している)

**Positive**
- I / We
  - will do
  - shall do
  - am / are going to do
- You / They / He / She / It
  - will do
  - are / is going to do

〜するでしょう
〜しましょう（shall）

**Negative**
- I / We
  - will not do
  - shall not do
  - am / are not going to do
- You / They / He / She / It
  - will not do
  - are / is not going to do

〜しないでしょう

**Question**
- Will / Shall — I / we do …?
- Am / Are — I / we going to do …?
- Will — you / they do …? / he / she / it do …?
- Are / Is — you / they going to do …? / he / she / it going to do …?

〜するでしょうか？
〜しましょうか？（shall）

過去　現在　未来

## 一般動詞　主語＋動詞

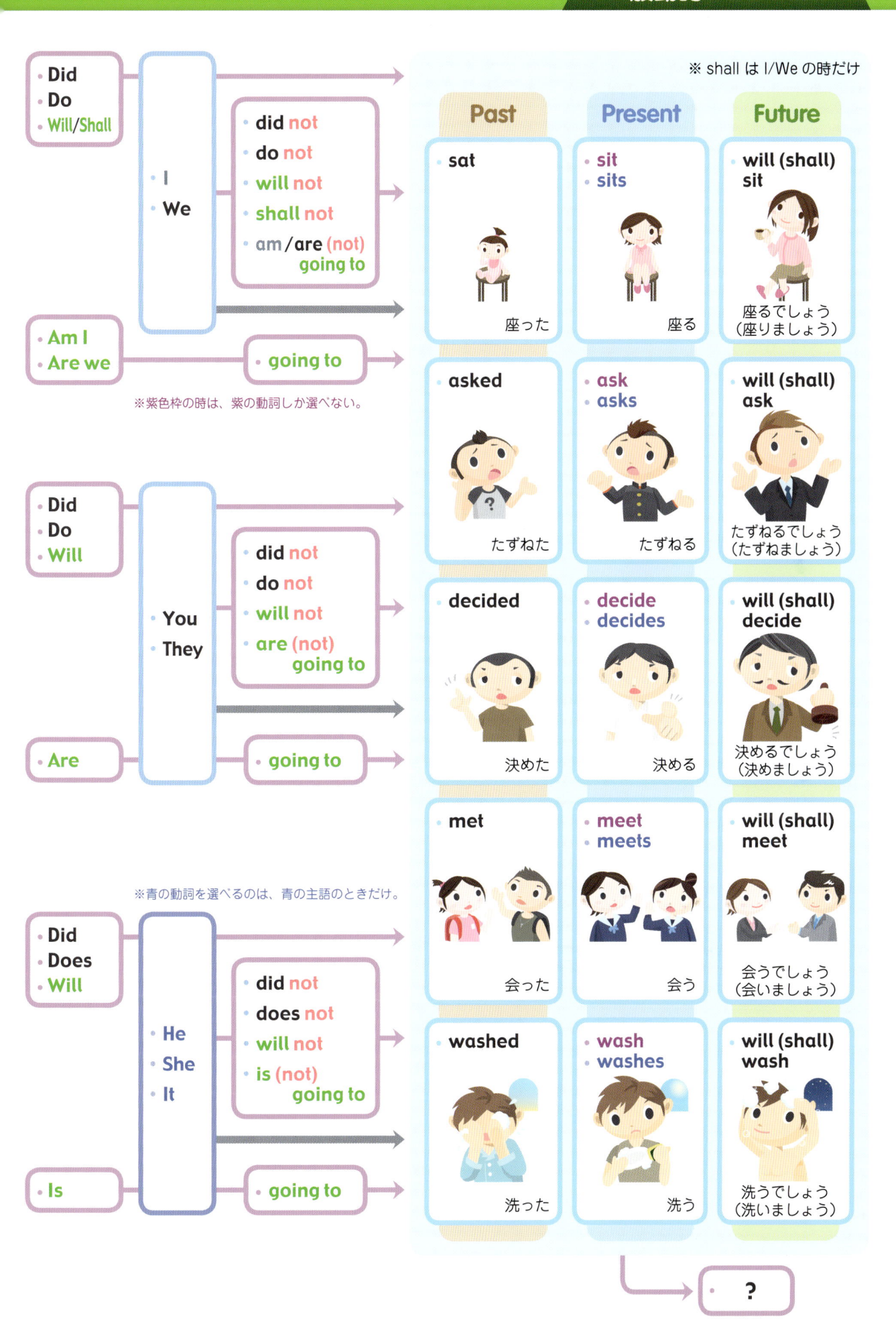

※ shall は I/We の時だけ

|  | Past | Present | Future |
|---|---|---|---|
| **Did / Do / Will/Shall** + **I / We** → **did not / do not / will not / shall not / am/are (not) going to** | sat 座った | sit / sits 座る | will (shall) sit 座るでしょう（座りましょう） |
| **Am I / Are we** → **going to** | | | |
| ※紫色枠の時は、紫の動詞しか選べない。 | asked たずねた | ask / asks たずねる | will (shall) ask たずねるでしょう（たずねましょう） |
| **Did / Do / Will** + **You / They** → **did not / do not / will not / are (not) going to** | decided 決めた | decide / decides 決める | will (shall) decide 決めるでしょう（決めましょう） |
| **Are** → **going to** | | | |
| | met 会った | meet / meets 会う | will (shall) meet 会うでしょう（会いましょう） |
| ※青の動詞を選べるのは、青の主語のときだけ。 | | | |
| **Did / Does / Will** + **He / She / It** → **did not / does not / will not / is (not) going to** | washed 洗った | wash / washes 洗う | will (shall) wash 洗うでしょう（洗いましょう） |
| **Is** → **going to** | | | |

? 

Part 2

twenty-one 21

# Simple Verb

## Practice / 練習

● 動詞を選んで中央に書き、その動詞を使って文章を作ろう。

※動詞の活用は、必要に応じて P.92〜95 を参考にしてね。
※最初に、黄色マスの文章を作成しよう。この形を基本にして、他の文章も作成しよう。

**myself** 自分自身

**I** 私

例）

|  | Past | Present | Future |
|---|---|---|---|
| **Positive** ○ | I watched TV. | I watch TV. | I will watch TV. |
| **Verb** 動詞 | | **watch** 見る | |
| **Negative** × | I did not watch TV. (didn't) | I do not watch TV. (don't) | I will not watch TV. (won't) |

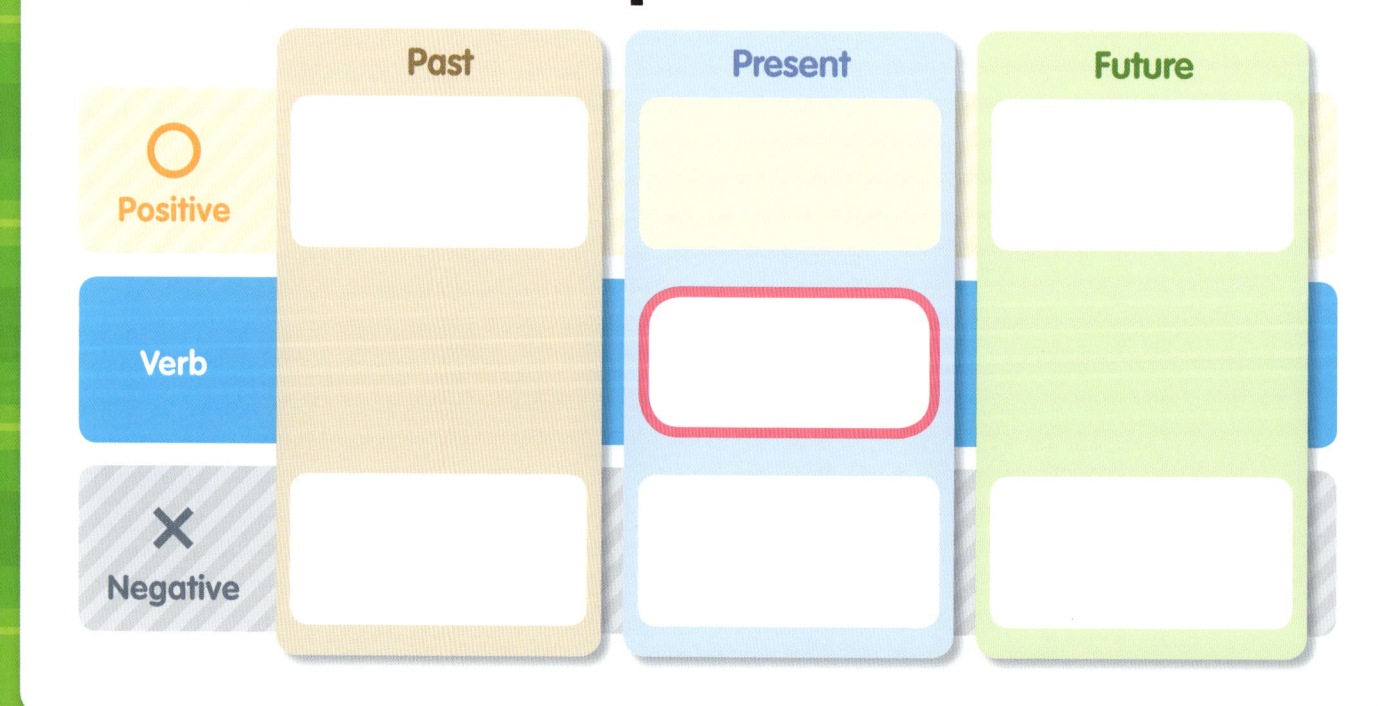

※ピンクの下線の動詞はすべて、中央の形と同じ「動詞の原形」を使用します。

**I**

|  | Past | Present | Future |
|---|---|---|---|
| **Positive** ○ | | | |
| **Verb** | | | |
| **Negative** × | | | |

Part 2

一般動詞　主語＋動詞

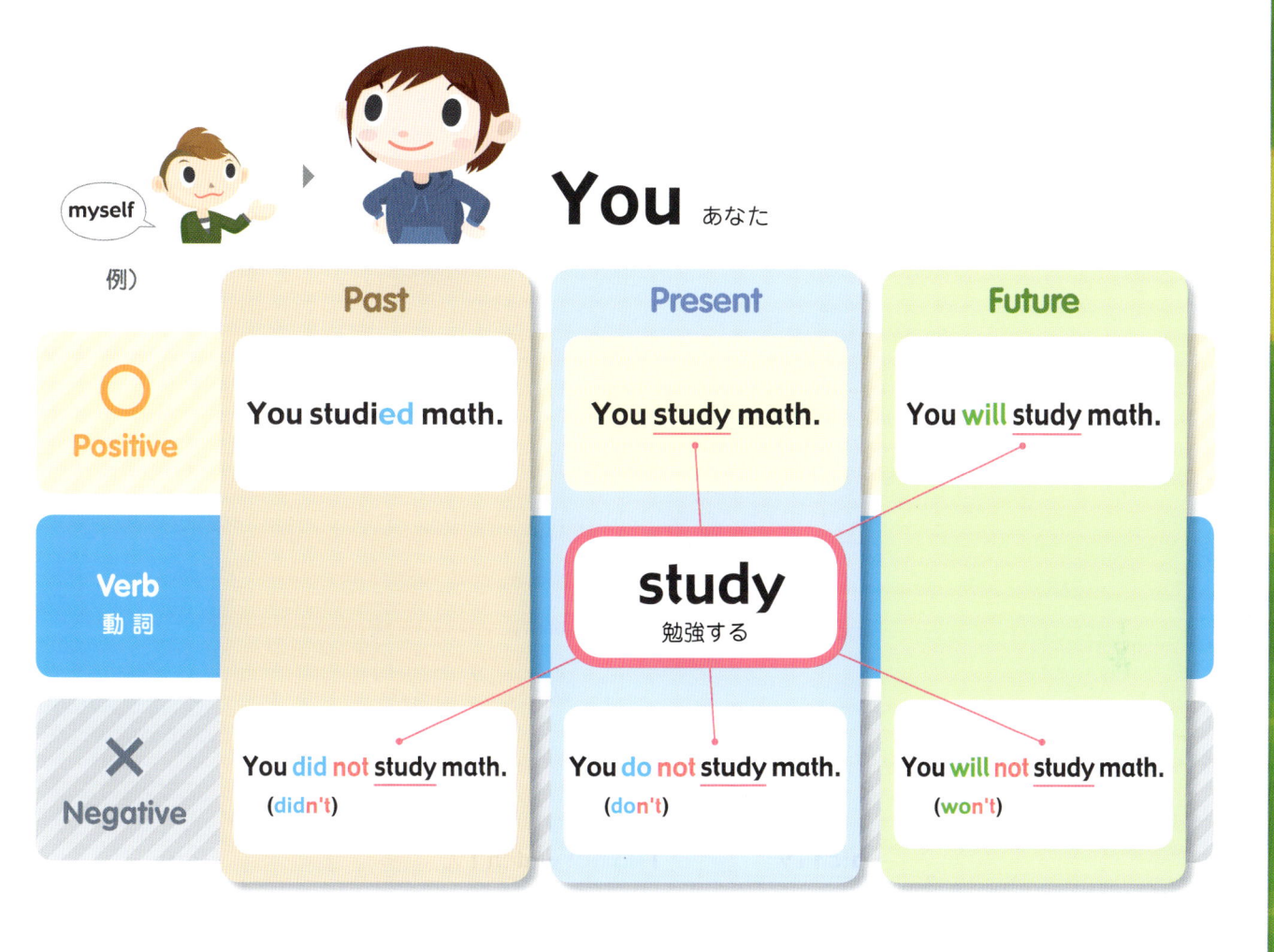

Part 2

例) myself ▶ **You** あなた

|  | Past | Present | Future |
|---|---|---|---|
| ○ Positive | You studi**ed** math. | You study math. | You **will** study math. |
| Verb 動詞 | | **study** 勉強する | |
| ✕ Negative | You **did not** study math. (**didn't**) | You **do not** study math. (**don't**) | You **will not** study math. (**won't**) |

**You**

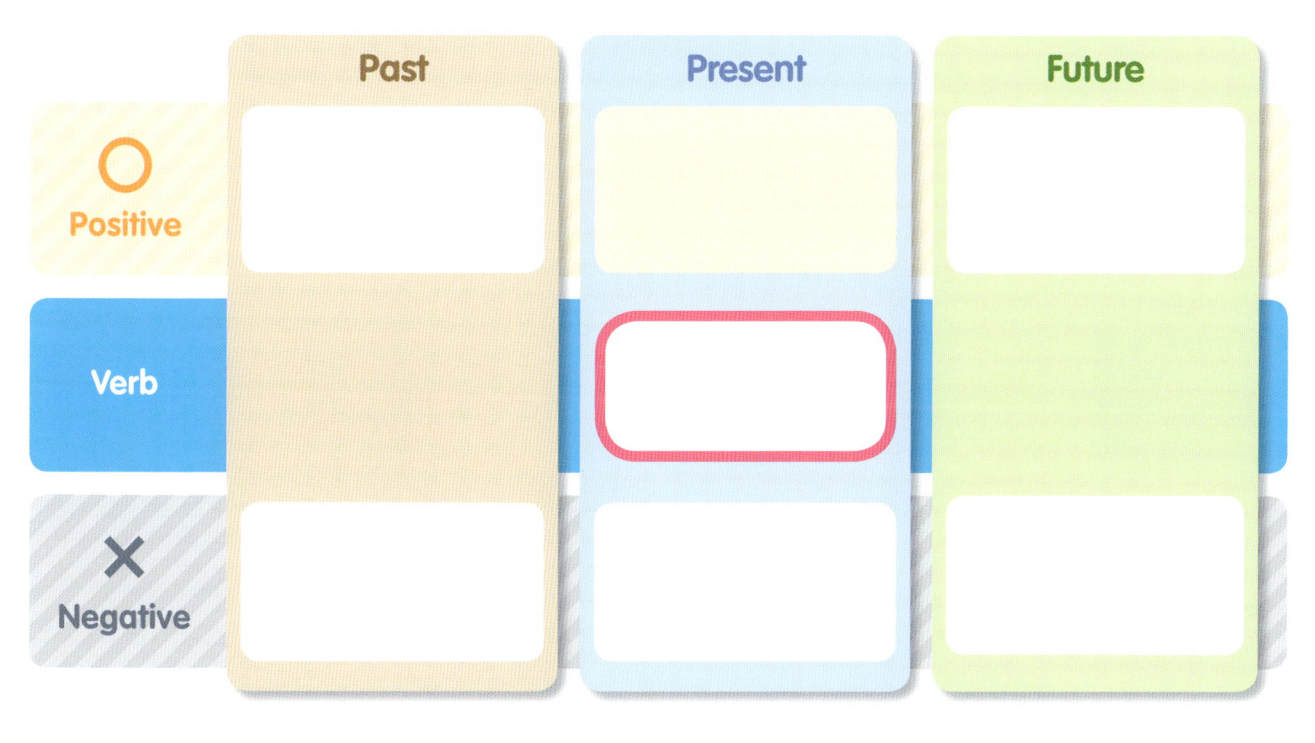

|  | Past | Present | Future |
|---|---|---|---|
| ○ Positive | | | |
| Verb | | | |
| ✕ Negative | | | |

twenty-three 23

## Simple Verb

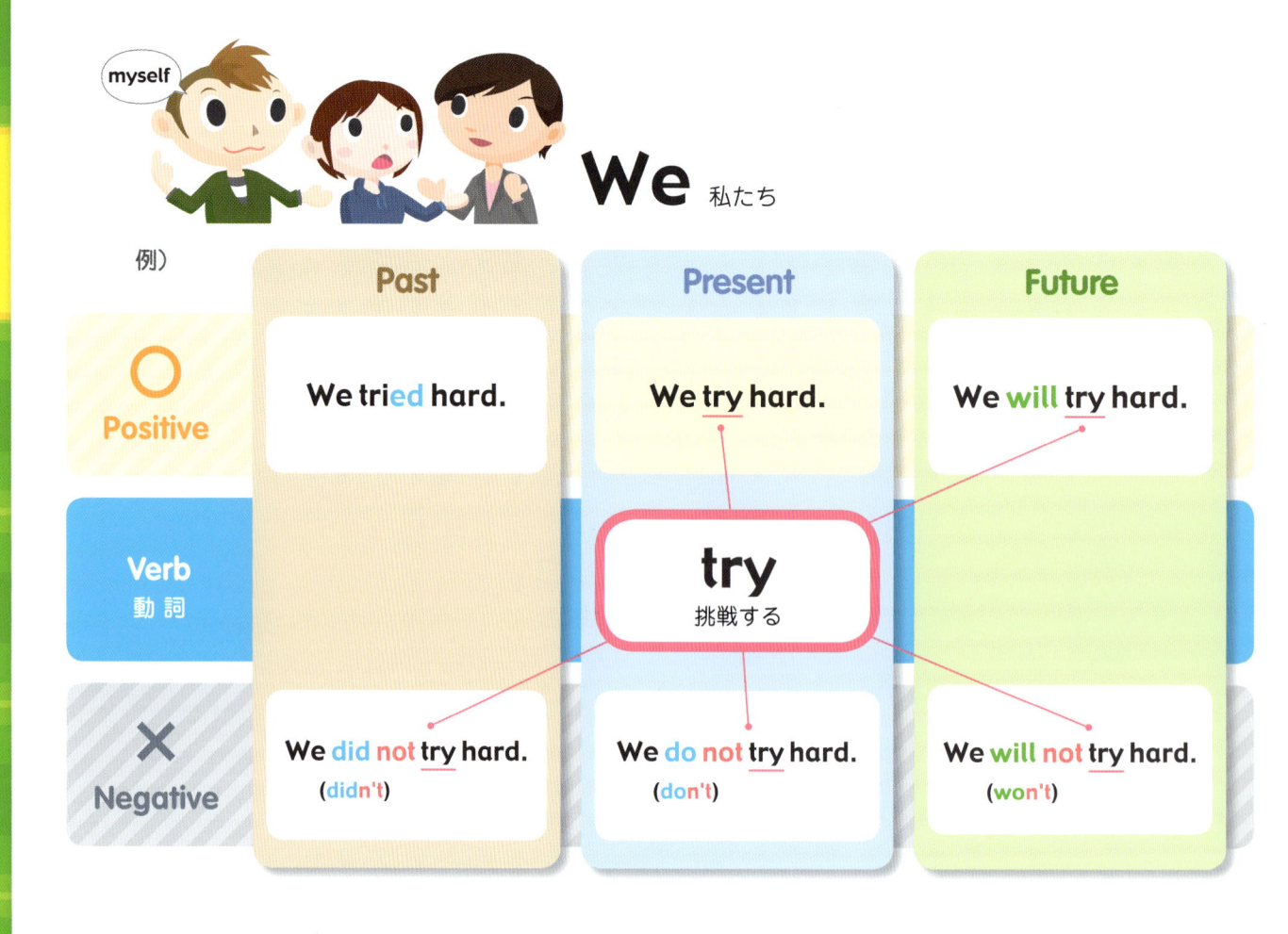

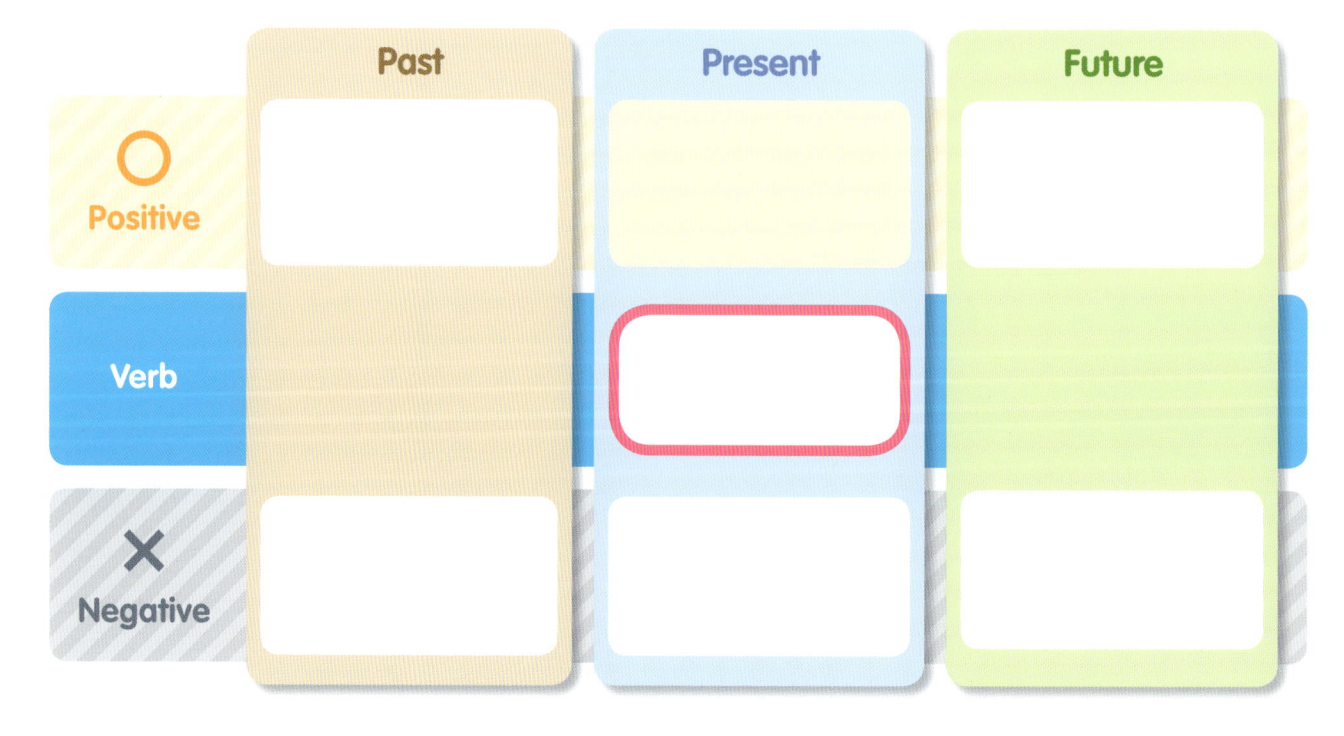

**Part 2**

myself

**We** 私たち

例）

**Positive** ○

|  | Past | Present | Future |
|---|---|---|---|
| Positive | We tri**ed** hard. | We try hard. | We **will** try hard. |
| Verb 動詞 | | **try** 挑戦する | |
| Negative | We **did not** try hard. (**didn't**) | We **do not** try hard. (**don't**) | We **will not** try hard. (**won't**) |

## We

|  | Past | Present | Future |
|---|---|---|---|
| Positive | | | |
| Verb | | | |
| Negative | | | |

24 twenty-four

一般動詞　主語 + 動詞

Part 2

## They 彼ら・彼女ら

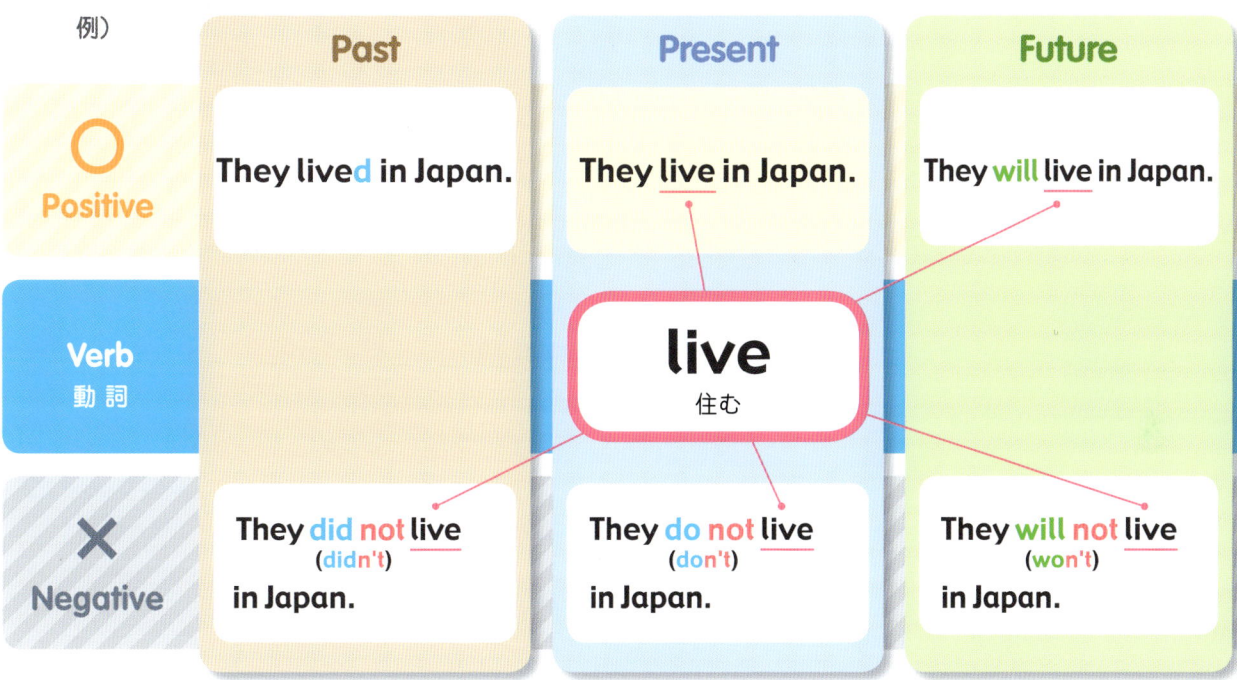

例）

|  | Past | Present | Future |
|---|---|---|---|
| Positive ○ | They lived in Japan. | They live in Japan. | They will live in Japan. |
| Verb 動詞 | | **live** 住む | |
| Negative × | They did not live (didn't) in Japan. | They do not live (don't) in Japan. | They will not live (won't) in Japan. |

## They

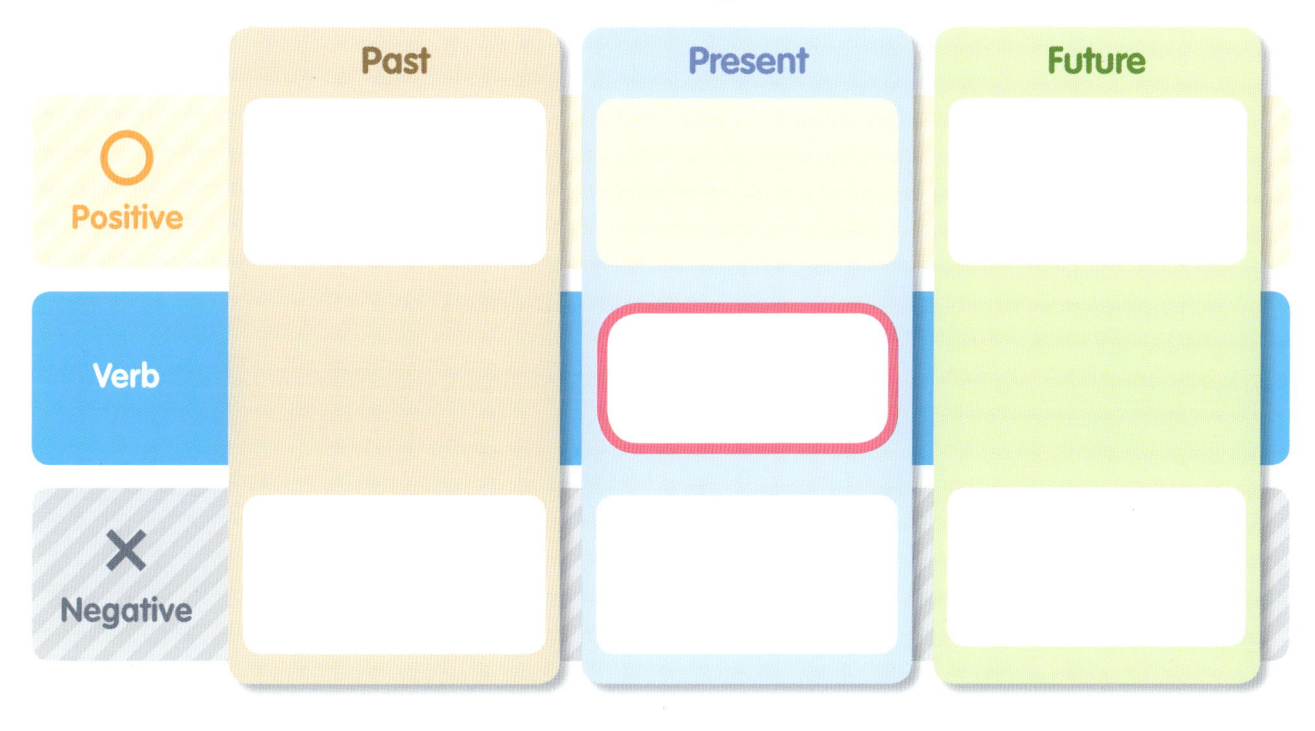

|  | Past | Present | Future |
|---|---|---|---|
| Positive ○ | | | |
| Verb | | | |
| Negative × | | | |

myself

twenty-five 25

## Simple Verb

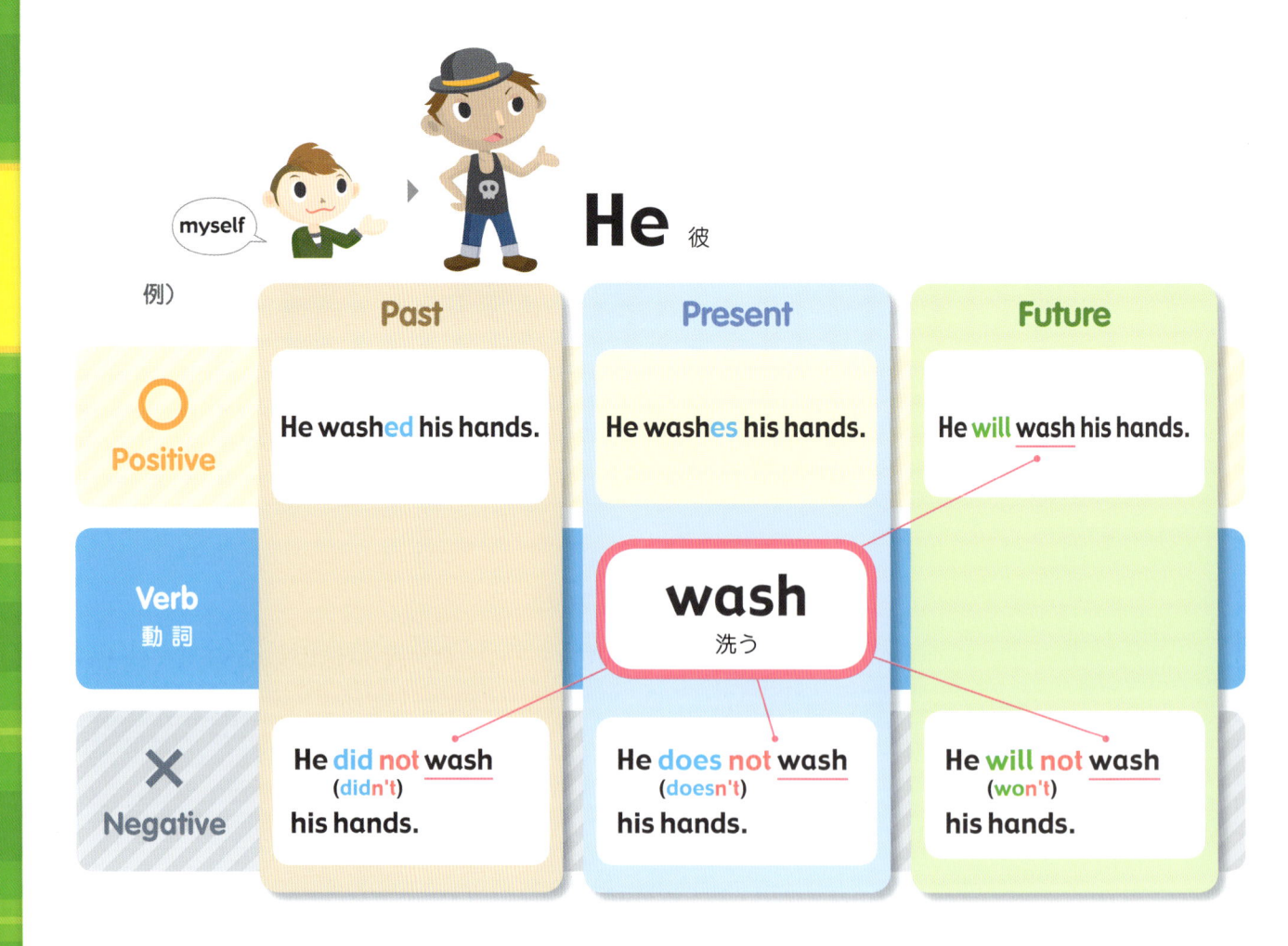

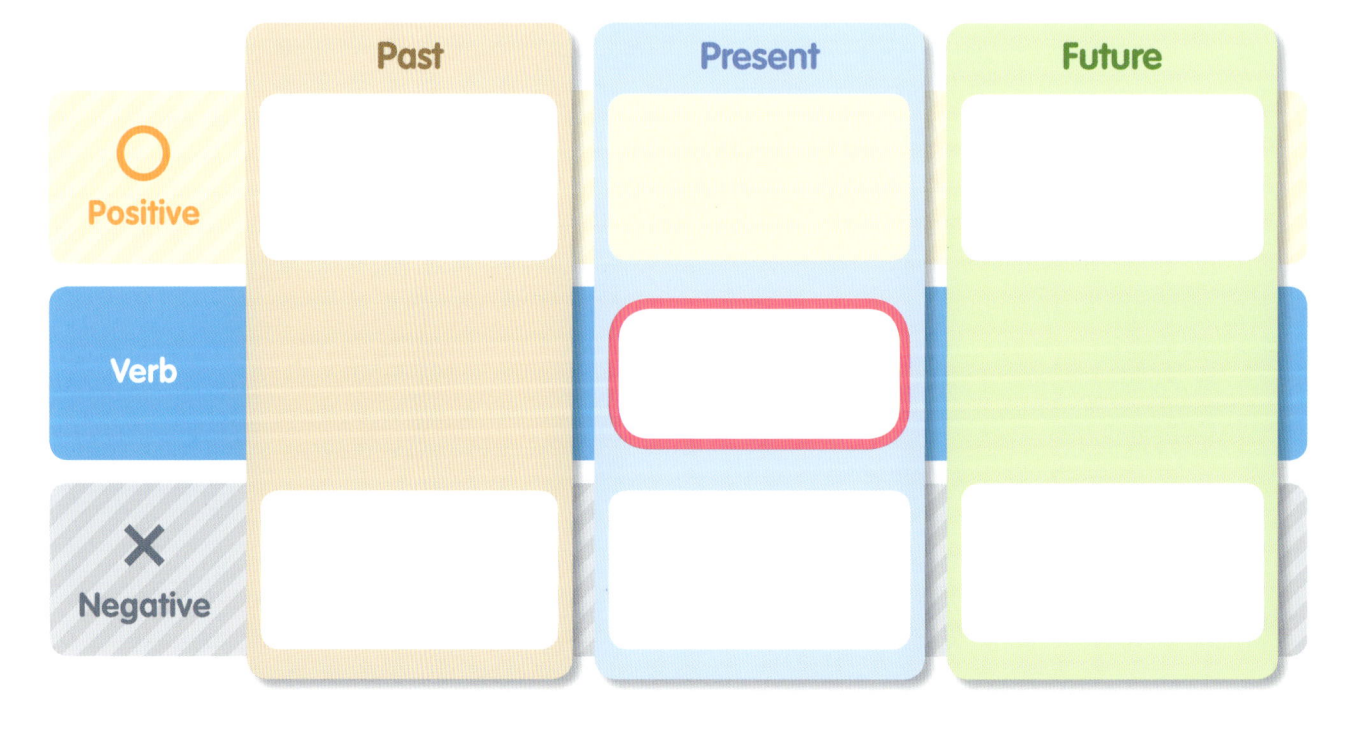

例) myself ▶ **He** 彼

|  | Past | Present | Future |
|---|---|---|---|
| ○ Positive | He wash**ed** his hands. | He wash**es** his hands. | He **will** wash his hands. |
| Verb 動詞 | | **wash** 洗う | |
| ✕ Negative | He **did not** wash (didn't) his hands. | He **does not** wash (doesn't) his hands. | He **will not** wash (won't) his hands. |

**He**

|  | Past | Present | Future |
|---|---|---|---|
| ○ Positive | | | |
| Verb | | | |
| ✕ Negative | | | |

Part 2

26 twenty-six

一般動詞　主語 + 動詞

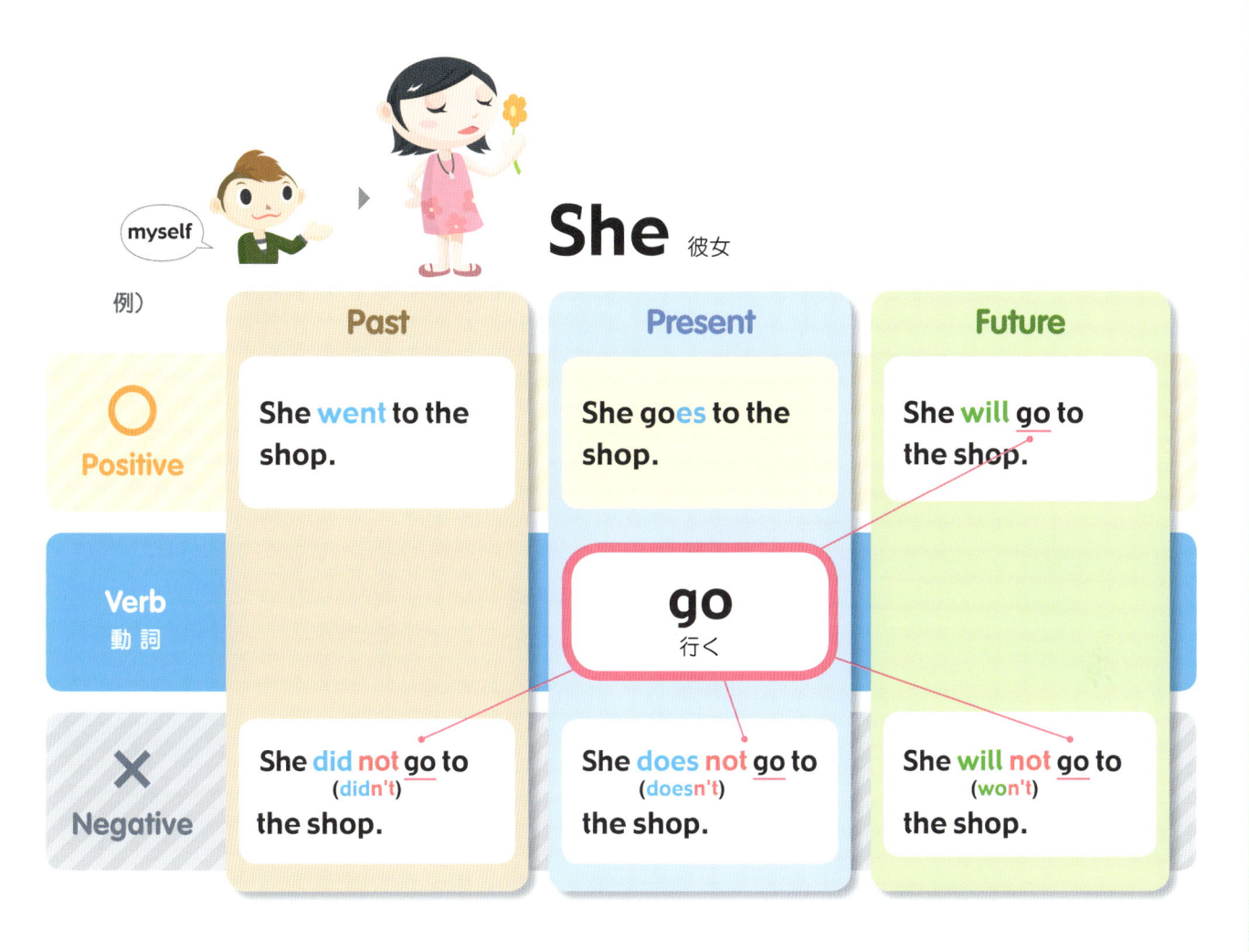

Part 2

myself ▶ **She** 彼女

|  | Past | Present | Future |
|---|---|---|---|
| ○ Positive | She went to the shop. | She goes to the shop. | She will go to the shop. |
| Verb 動詞 | | **go** 行く | |
| ✕ Negative | She did not (didn't) go to the shop. | She does not (doesn't) go to the shop. | She will not (won't) go to the shop. |

**She**

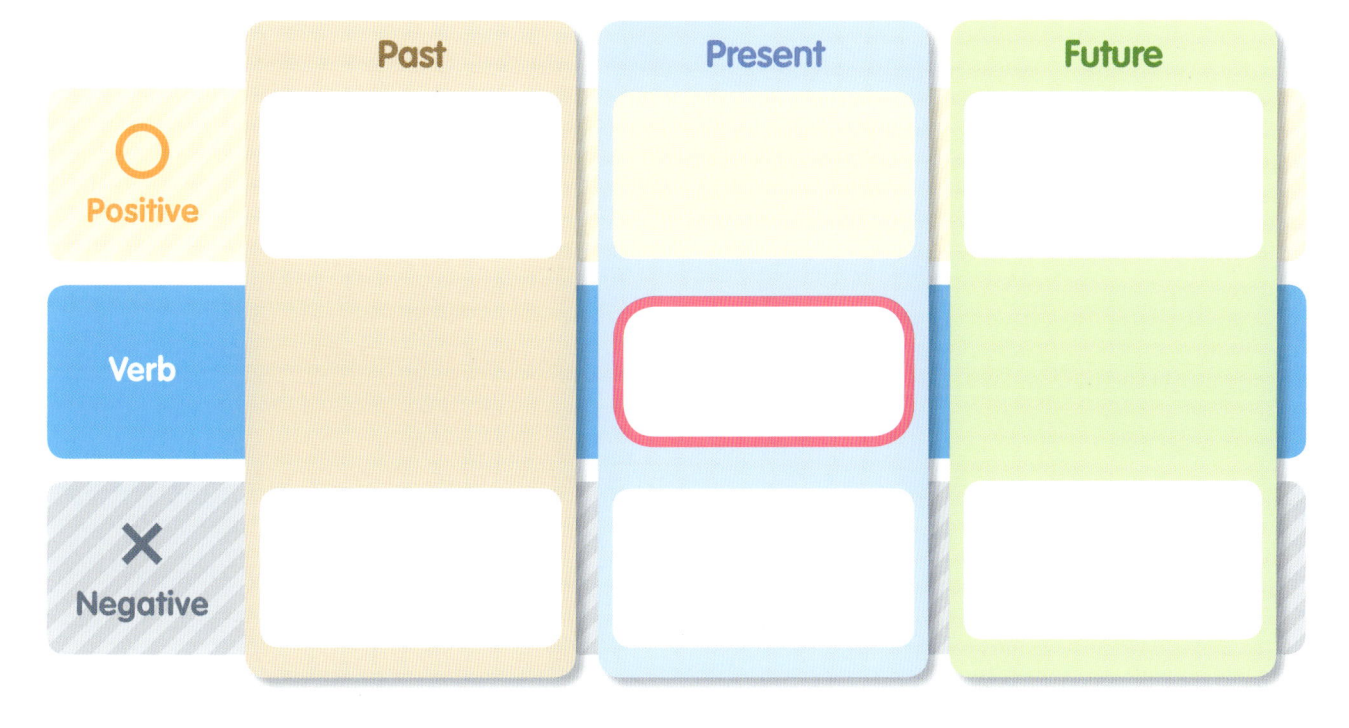

|  | Past | Present | Future |
|---|---|---|---|
| ○ Positive | | | |
| Verb | | | |
| ✕ Negative | | | |

twenty-seven 27

## Simple Verb

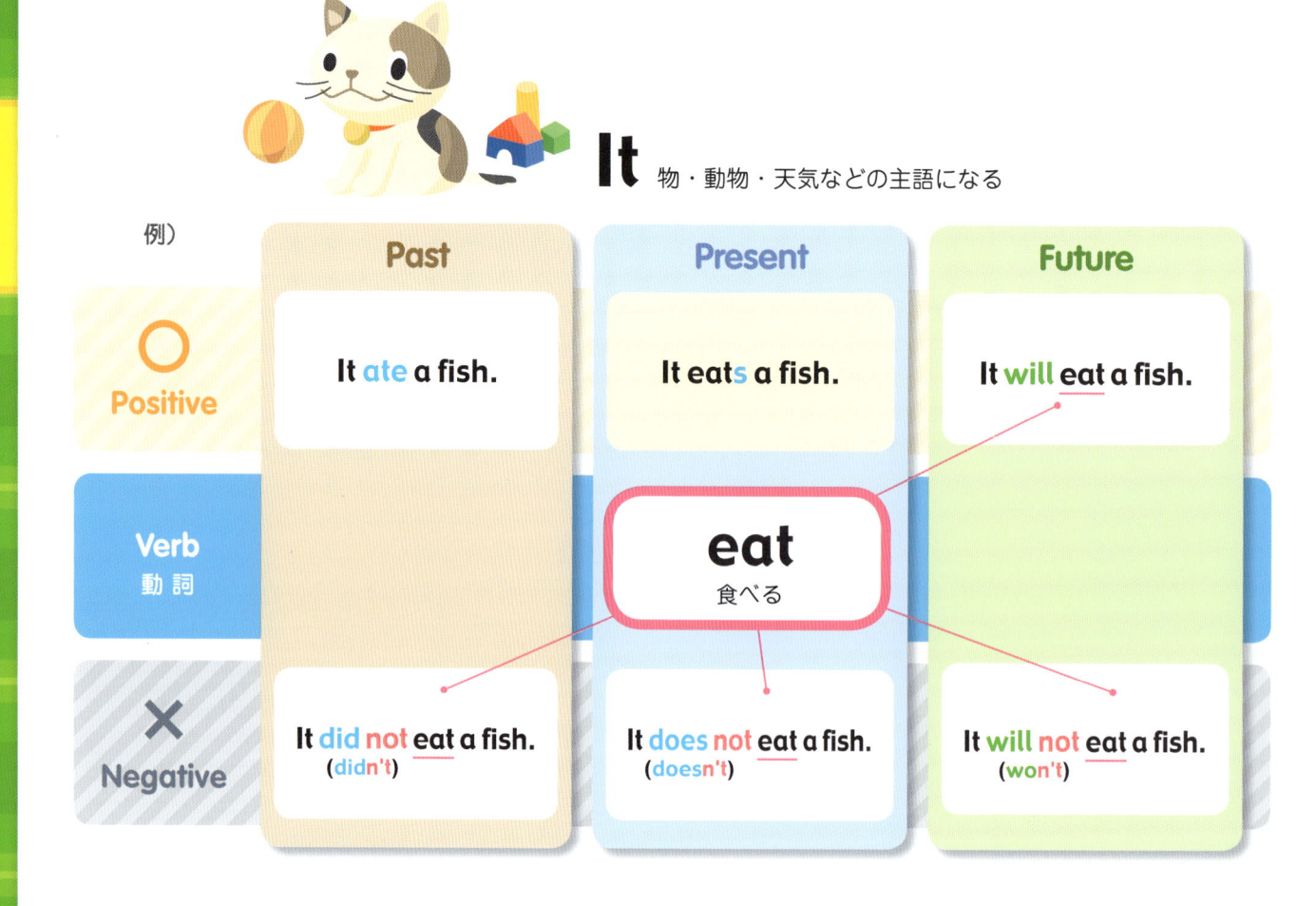

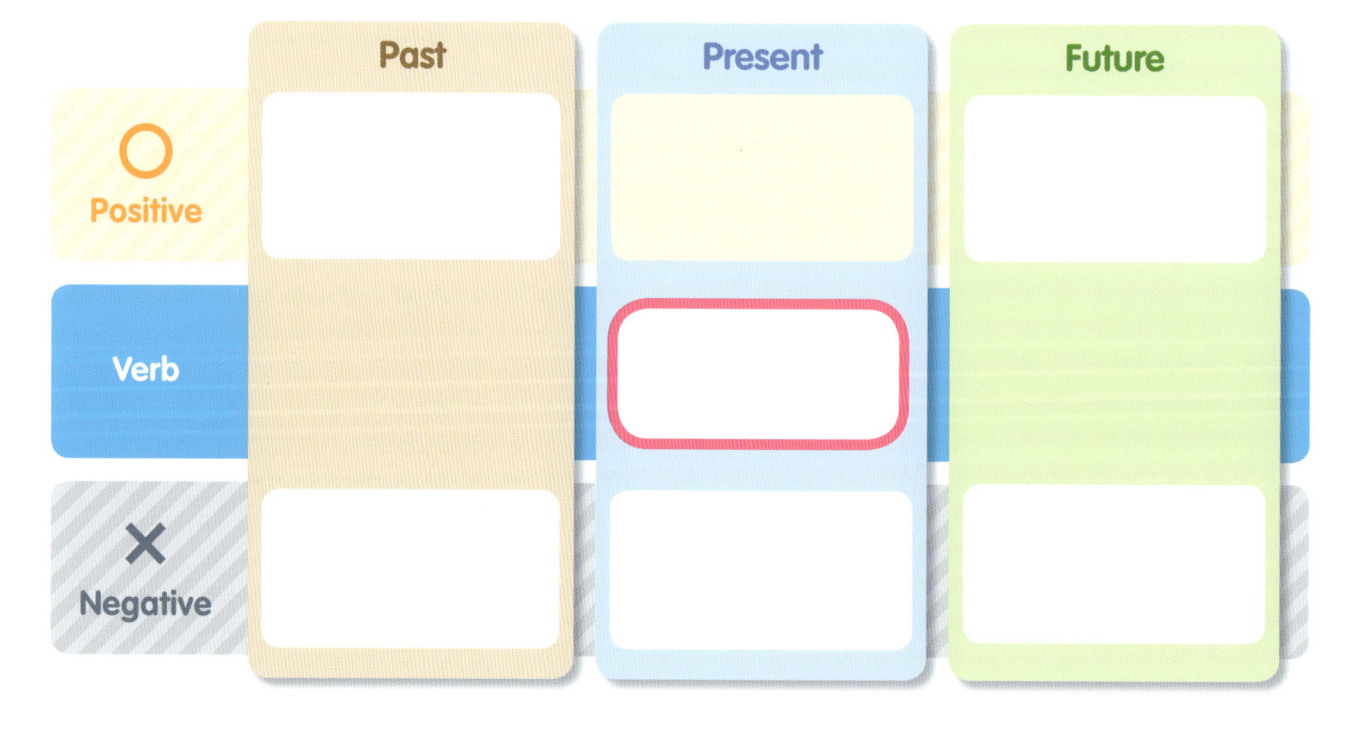

**Part 2**

It 物・動物・天気などの主語になる

例）

| | Past | Present | Future |
|---|---|---|---|
| ○ Positive | It ate a fish. | It eats a fish. | It will eat a fish. |
| Verb 動詞 | | **eat** 食べる | |
| × Negative | It did not eat a fish. (didn't) | It does not eat a fish. (doesn't) | It will not eat a fish. (won't) |

## It

| | Past | Present | Future |
|---|---|---|---|
| ○ Positive | | | |
| Verb | | | |
| × Negative | | | |

28 twenty-eight

一般動詞　主語＋動詞

## Practice Test / 確認テスト

| ！ 動詞ヒント | • stay 泊まる | • fly 飛ぶ | • meet 会う |
| | • wash 洗う | • like 好き | |

**Part 2**

① 次の文を現在形から過去形にしてみよう。　　　　　　　　　　　　　　　※解答は P.57

例) I <u>study</u> <u>English</u>.　☞　I <u>studied</u> English.
　　　勉強する　英　語　　　　　　勉強した

1. You <u>stay</u> at your friend's <u>house</u>.　☞　You _____ at your friend's house.
　　　　　　　　　あなたの友達の家

2. He <u>flies</u> <u>back to Tokyo</u>.　☞　_____
　　　　　　　東京へ帰る


② 次の文を現在形から未来形にしてみよう。

例) I <u>sit</u> on the <u>chair</u>.　☞　I <u>will</u> <u>sit</u> on the chair.
　　座る　　　　イス

1. You <u>meet</u> my <u>mother</u>.　☞　You _____ my mother.
　　　　　　　　お母さん

2. He <u>washes</u> his <u>hands</u>.　☞　_____
　　　　　　　両手


③ 次の文を肯定から疑問にしてみよう。

例) You <u>go</u> to <u>school</u>.　☞　Do you <u>go</u> to school?
　　　行く　　学校

1. They <u>wash</u> their <u>car</u>.　☞　_____ they <u>wash</u> their car?
　　　　　　　　　車

2. She <u>likes</u> <u>fruit</u>.　☞　_____
　　　　　　　果物

## Simple Verb

### Diary / えいご日記

**Setsubun** (Bean-Throwing Festival) 節分

● 下線部に適切な語句を記入して、えいご日記を完成させよう。　　※解答は P.57

Part 2

**Today** is "Setsubun".
今日

**This year's lucky direction** is **South-East**.
　　今年の恵方　　　　　　　　　　南東

I _____ an **ogre mask** _____ **day(s) ago**.
　作った　　　鬼のお面　　（数字）　日　　前

My **father** _____ the ogre and **scared us**.
　お父さん　　　演じた　　　　　　　私たちを恐がらせた

I _____ **lots of beans** at the ogre and **scared him away**.
　投げた　　　たくさんの豆　　　　　　　　彼を恐がらせて追い出した

I _____ **dinner** without **saying anything**.
　食べた　　夕食　　　　　ひとことも言わないで

> ! ヒント　　• **make** 作る　　• **play** 演じる　　• **throw** 投げる　　• **eat** 食べる

● 上の文章を絵に描いてみよう。

一般動詞　主語＋動詞

● 左ページのえいご日記を書き写そう。

## Question

● 質問に答えよう。その答えを下に書き写そう。

1. <u>Who</u> <u>made</u> an ogre mask?
   　誰　　作った
   ☞ _____ made an ogre mask.

2. Did you <u>throw</u> lots of beans?
   　　　　投げる
   ☞　Yes, _____ did. / No, _____ did not.

3. Did you <u>speak</u> during dinner?
   　　　　話す
   ☞　Yes, _____ did. / No, _____ did not.

## Simple Verb

● 文章を自分で作ってみよう。

# Part 3

# 進行形
## Continuous

主語（私は・あなたは…など）が
「〜をしている」と表現する時に使う動詞です。

## Continuous

# ● 進行形

**主語 + be 動詞 + doing**

|  | **Past** 過去 | **Present** 現在 | **Future** 未来 |
|---|---|---|---|
| **○ Positive 肯定** | • I was<br>• You / We / They were<br>• He / She / It was<br>└ • doing<br>〜していた | • I am<br>• You / We / They are<br>• He / She / It is<br>└ • doing<br>〜しています | • I / We ─ • will be doing / • shall be doing<br>• You / They / He / She / It<br>└ • will be doing<br>〜しているでしょう |
| **✕ Negative 否定** | • I was<br>• You / We / They were<br>• He / She / It was<br>└ • not doing<br>〜していませんでした | • I am<br>• You / We / They are<br>• He / She / It is<br>└ • not doing<br>〜していません | • I / We ─ • will not be doing / • shall not be doing<br>• You / They / He / She / It<br>└ • will not be doing<br>〜していないでしょう |
| **? Question 疑問** | • Was I<br>• Were you / we / they<br>• Was he / she / it<br>└ • doing … ?<br>〜していましたか？ | • Am I<br>• Are you / we / they<br>• Is he / she / it<br>└ • doing … ?<br>〜していますか？ | • Will / Shall I / we<br>• Will you / they<br>• Will he / she / it<br>└ • be doing … ?<br>〜しているでしょうか？ |

過去　現在　未来

Part 3

34 thirty-four

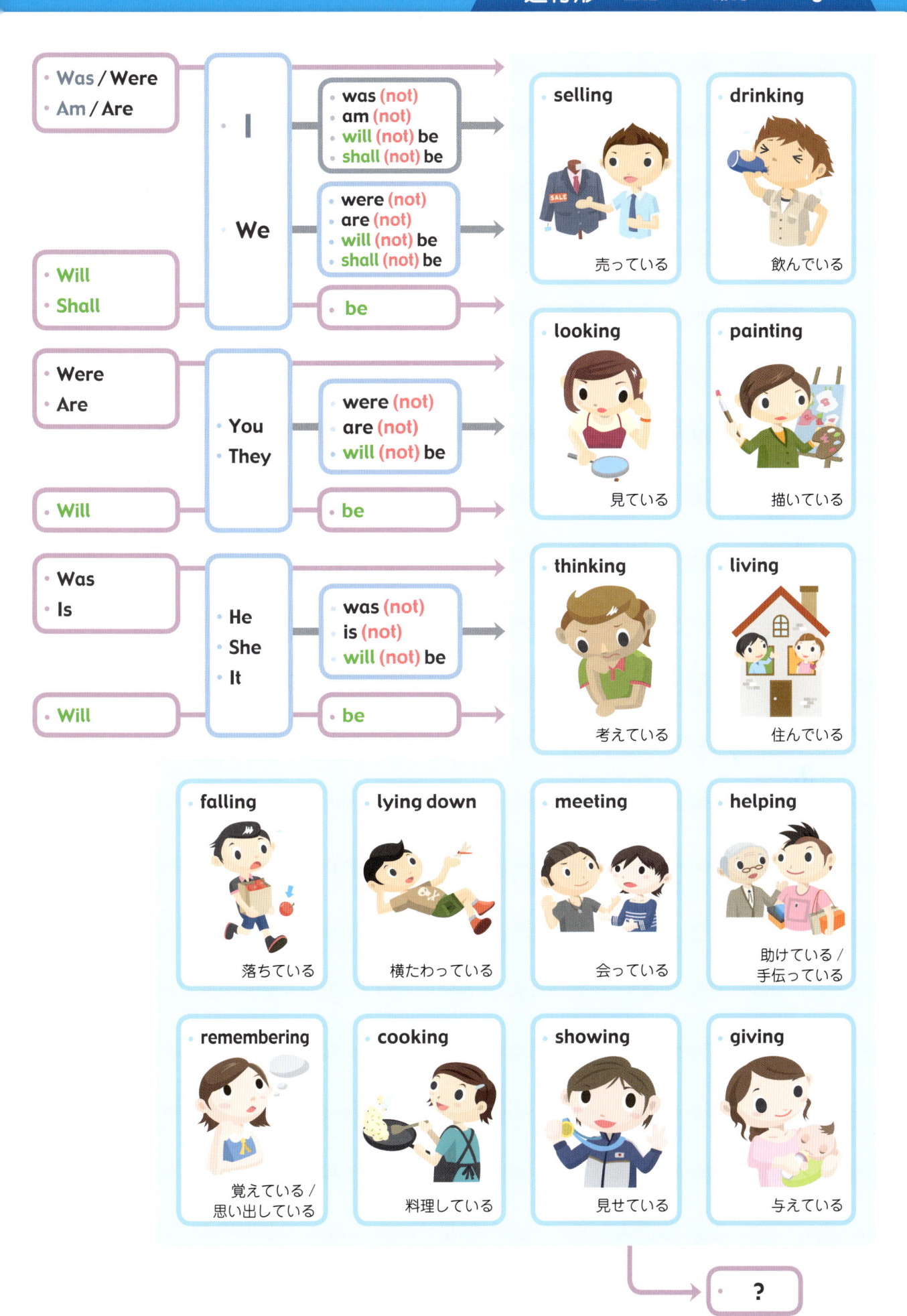

## 進行形　主語 + be動詞 + doing

**Part 3**

- Was / Were
- Am / Are

- I
  - was (not)
  - am (not)
  - will (not) be
  - shall (not) be

- We
  - were (not)
  - are (not)
  - will (not) be
  - shall (not) be

- Will
- Shall
  - be

- Were
- Are

- You / They
  - were (not)
  - are (not)
  - will (not) be

- Will
  - be

- Was
- Is

- He / She / It
  - was (not)
  - is (not)
  - will (not) be

- Will
  - be

- selling　売っている
- drinking　飲んでいる
- looking　見ている
- painting　描いている
- thinking　考えている
- living　住んでいる
- falling　落ちている
- lying down　横たわっている
- meeting　会っている
- helping　助けている / 手伝っている
- remembering　覚えている / 思い出している
- cooking　料理している
- showing　見せている
- giving　与えている
- ?

thirty-five 35

## Continuous

### Practice / 練習

- P.34〜35を参考に、自分で文章を作成してみよう。

**Part 3**

**現在形**
I am _____.

I am not _____.

**過去形**
I was _____.

I was not _____.

**未来形**
I will be _____.

I will not be _____.

**疑問形**
Are you _____?

Were you _____?

Will you be _____?

## Practice Test / 確認テスト

進行形　主語 + be動詞 + doing

| ! 動詞ヒント | • watch 見る | • cook 料理する | • feed エサをやる |
|---|---|---|---|
| | • draw 描く | • study 勉強する | • live 住む |

① 次の文を肯定から進行形にしてみよう。　　※解答は P.57

例) He <u>sells</u> books.　☞　He <u>is selling</u> books.
　　　売る　　　　　　　　　　　売っている

1. I <u>watch</u> TV.　☞　I _____ TV.

2. You <u>cook</u> my dinner.　☞　_____

② 次の文を肯定から否定にしてみよう。

例) He <u>is helping</u> his <u>mother</u>.　☞　He <u>is</u> <u>not</u> <u>helping</u> his mother.
　　　手伝っている　お母さん

1. We <u>are feeding</u> the cat.　☞　We _____ the cat.

2. He <u>is drawing</u> a <u>picture</u>.　☞　_____
　　　　　　　　　　絵

③ 次の文を肯定から疑問にしてみよう。

例) Kosuke <u>is eating</u> an <u>apple</u>.　☞　<u>Is</u> Kosuke <u>eating</u> an apple?
　　　　　　食べている　　リンゴ

1. You <u>are studying</u> <u>mathematics</u>.　☞　_____ you _____ mathematics?
　　　　　　　　　　　　　算数

2. They <u>are living</u> in London.　☞　_____

Part 3

## Continuous

### Diary / えいご日記

**Boys' Festival**
こどもの日

● 下線部に適切な語句を記入して、えいご日記を完成させよう。　　※解答は P.57

_____ is Boys' Festival.
　今　日

I am _____ a chimaki and _____ this diary.
　　　食べている　　　　　ちまき　　　　　　書いている　　　日記

My father is _____ carp streamers outside for me.
　　　　　　つり下げている　　　こいのぼり　　　　　外　　私のために

It is as if they are _____ in the sky.
　　　まるで　　　　　泳いでいる　　　　空で

I _____ May the most because I _____ carp streamers,
　好き　　　　5月　　一番　　　　　　　　好き

chimaki and kashiwamochi.
　　　　　　　柏餅

| ！ヒント | • today 今日　• eat 食べる　• write 書く |
|---|---|
|  | • hang つり下げる　• swim 泳ぐ　• like 好き |

● 上の文章を絵に描いてみよう。

進行形　主語 + be動詞 + doing

● 左ページの日記を書き写そう。

Part 3

## Question

● 質問に答えよう。その答えを下に書き写そう。

1. <u>What</u> festival is it today?
   何

   ☞　Today is _____ .

2. <u>Who</u> is hanging carp streamers?
   誰

   ☞　_____ is hanging carp streamers.

3. <u>What</u> are you <u>doing</u>?
   何　　　　している

   ☞　I am _____ a chimaki and _____ this diary.

thirty-nine 39

## Continuous

- 文章を自分で作ってみよう。

# Part 4

## 受動態
Passive

主語（私は・あなたは…など）が「〜される」と表現する時に使う文法です。

## Passive

# 受動態

**主語 ＋ be 動詞 ＋ done**

※ "done" に入る単語は、動詞の最後に "ed" を付けるか、P.94～95「不規則動詞変化表」の過去分詞から選ぶ。

Part 4

|  | **Past** 過去 | **Present** 現在 | **Future** 未来 |
|---|---|---|---|
| **○ Positive** 肯定 | ・I was<br>・You / We / They were<br>・He / She / It was<br>　└ ・done<br>〜された | ・I am<br>・You / We / They are<br>・He / She / It is<br>　└ ・done<br>〜される | ・I / We ─ ・will be done / ・shall be done<br>・You / They<br>・He / She / It<br>　└ ・will be done<br>〜されるでしょう |
| **× Negative** 否定 | ・I was<br>・You / We / They were<br>・He / She / It was<br>　└ ・not done<br>〜されなかった | ・I am<br>・You / We / They are<br>・He / She / It is<br>　└ ・not done<br>〜されない | ・I / We ─ ・will not be done / ・shall not be done<br>・You / They<br>・He / She / It<br>　└ ・will not be done<br>〜されないでしょう |
| **? Question** 疑問 | ・Was I<br>・Were you / we / they<br>・Was he / she / it<br>　└ ・done ... ?<br>〜されましたか？ | ・Am I<br>・Are you / we / they<br>・Is he / she / it<br>　└ ・done ... ?<br>〜されますか？ | ・Will / Shall I<br>・Will / Shall we<br>・Will you / they<br>・Will he / she / it<br>　└ ・be done ... ?<br>〜されるでしょうか？ |

過去　現在　未来

## 受動態　主語 + be動詞 + done

- Was / Were
- Am / Are

- I
- We

- was (not)
- were (not)
- am (not)
- are (not)
- will (not) be
- shall (not) be

- Will
- Shall

- be

- Were
- Are

- You
- They

- were (not)
- are (not)
- will (not) be

- Will

- be

- Was
- Is

- He
- She
- It

- was (not)
- is (not)
- will (not) be

- Will

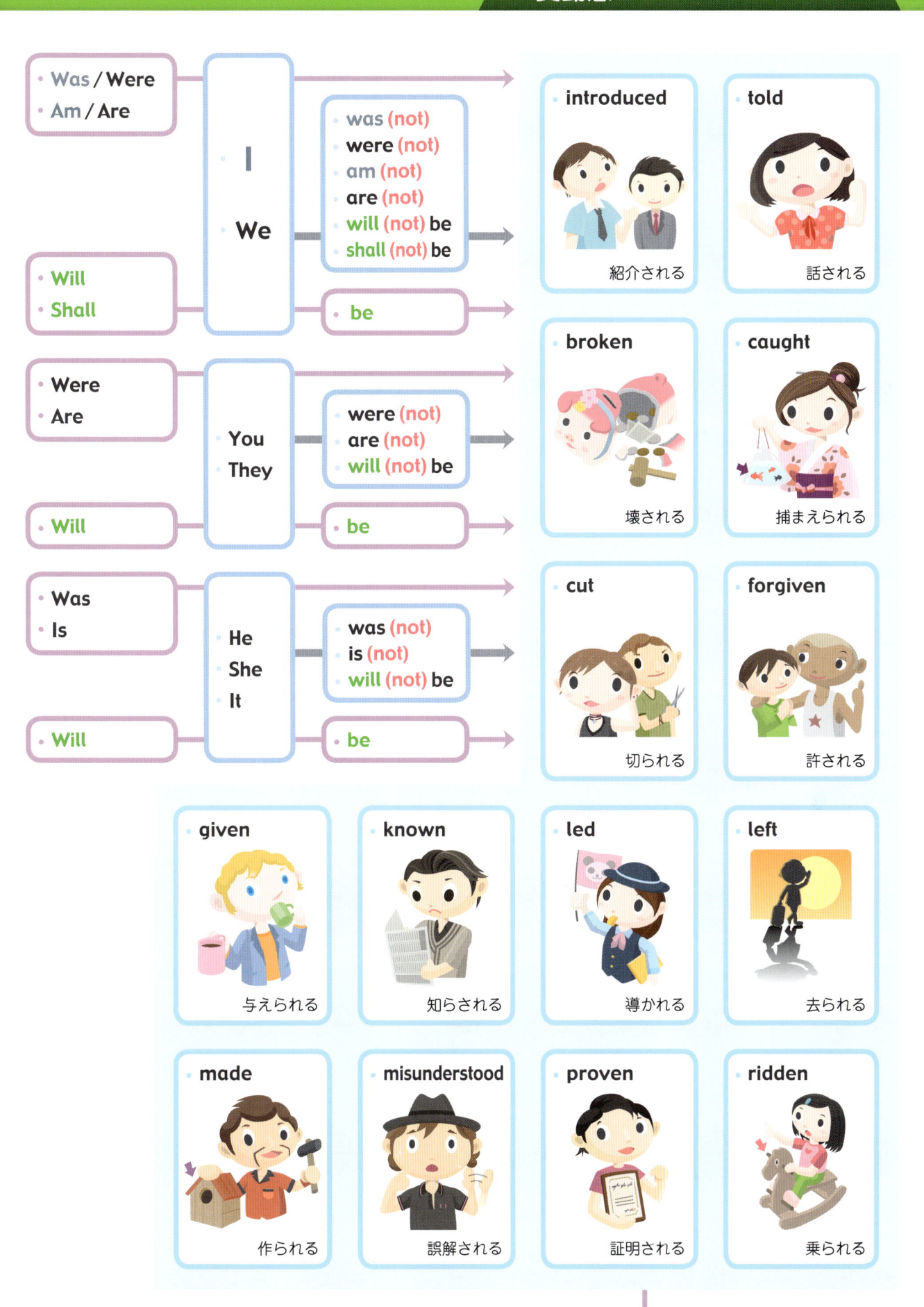

- be

- introduced — 紹介される
- told — 話される
- broken — 壊される
- caught — 捕まえられる
- cut — 切られる
- forgiven — 許される
- given — 与えられる
- known — 知らされる
- led — 導かれる
- left — 去られる
- made — 作られる
- misunderstood — 誤解される
- proven — 証明される
- ridden — 乗られる

※紫色枠の時は、最後の「.」を取る。

- ?

Part 4

## Passive

### Practice / 練習

● P.42〜43を参考に、自分で文章を作成してみよう。

**現在形**

I am _____ .

I am not _____ .

**過去形**

I was _____ .

I was not _____ .

**未来形**

I will be _____ .

I will not be _____ .

**疑問形**

Are you _____ ?

Were you _____ ?

Will you be _____ ?

## 受動態　主語 + be動詞 + done

## Practice Test / 確認テスト

!  動詞ヒント
- show 見せる
- make 作る
- introduce 紹介する
- tell 話す
- give 与える
- ride 乗る

### ① 次の文を能動態から受動態にしてみよう。

※解答は P.57

例）My friend gives me candy. ☞ I am given candy by my friend.
　　私の友達　与える　私に　キャンディー　　　　与えられた　　　　友達から

1. His father shows him the way. ☞ He _____ the way by his father.
　　　　　　　　　彼に

2. She introduces me to her father. ☞ _____

### ② 次の文を肯定から否定にしてみよう。

例）He is helped by his mother. ☞ He is not helped by his mother.
　　　　手伝わされる　　お母さん

1. You are given money by your family. ☞ You _____ money by your family.
　　　　　　　　お金　　家族から

2. It is made in India. ☞ _____

### ③ 次の文を現在形から過去形にしてみよう。

例）He is left by his friend. ☞ He was left by his friend.
　　　去られる　　　　　　　　　　　　去られた

1. She is told to go to university. ☞ She _____ to go to university.
　　　　　　　　　　　大学

2. The horse is ridden by me. ☞ _____
　　　馬

Part 4

## Passive

### Diary / えいご日記 — The Rainy Season 梅雨

● 下線部に適切な語句を記入して、えいご日記を完成させよう。　※解答は P.57

It will <u>rain</u> a lot <u>this month</u>.
　　　　雨

This season _____ the _____.
　　　　　　　　呼ばれる　　　　　　　　　梅雨

On the way to school, I can see many hydrangeas, frogs and snails.
行く途中　　　　　　　　　　　　　多くの　　アジサイ　　カエル　　カタツムリ

It seems like they are happy in the rain.
ように見える　　　　　楽しんでいる　　雨の中

_____ and _____ _____ by us.
　カエル　　　　　カタツムリ　　　捕まえられる　　私たちに

_____ _____ by us.　They bring us joy.
　アジサイ　　　　　　採られる　　　　　　　　　　　　　　　喜び

> !ヒント　　・call 呼ぶ　　・catch 捕まえる　　・take 採る

● 上の文章を絵に描いてみよう。

受動態　主語 + be動詞 + done

● 左ページの日記を書き写そう。

## Question

● 質問に答えよう。その答えを下に書き写そう。

1. <u>What</u> is the season called?
   何

   ☞　This season is called the _____.

2. Is there <u>a lot of</u> rain?
           たくさん

   ☞　Yes, there is. / No, there is not.

3. What did you <u>find</u> on the way to school?
                 見つける

   ☞　I found _____, _____ and _____.

Part 4

## Passive

● 文章を自分で作ってみよう。

# Part 5

# 受動態 進行形
## Passive Continuous

主語（私は・あなたは…など）が
「〜され続けている」と表現する時に使う文法です。

## Passive Continuous

# 受動態 進行形

主語 + be 動詞 + being + done

|  | **Past** 過去 | **Present** 現在 | **Future** 未来 |
|---|---|---|---|
| **Positive** 肯定 | • I was<br>• You / We / They were<br>• He / She / It was<br>└ • being done<br>〜され続けていた | • I am<br>• You / We / They are<br>• He / She / It is<br>└ • being done<br>〜され続けている | ※文法上は可能だが、実生活においてはあまり使用されない。 |
| **Negative** 否定 | • I was<br>• You / We / They were<br>• He / She / It was<br>└ • not being done<br>〜され続けていなかった | • I am<br>• You / We / They are<br>• He / She / It is<br>└ • not being done<br>〜され続けていない | |
| **Question** 疑問 | • Was I<br>• Were you / we / they<br>• Was he / she / it<br>└ • being done …?<br>〜され続けていましたか？ | • Am I<br>• Are you / we / they<br>• Is he / she / it<br>└ • being done …?<br>〜され続けていますか？ | |

Part 5

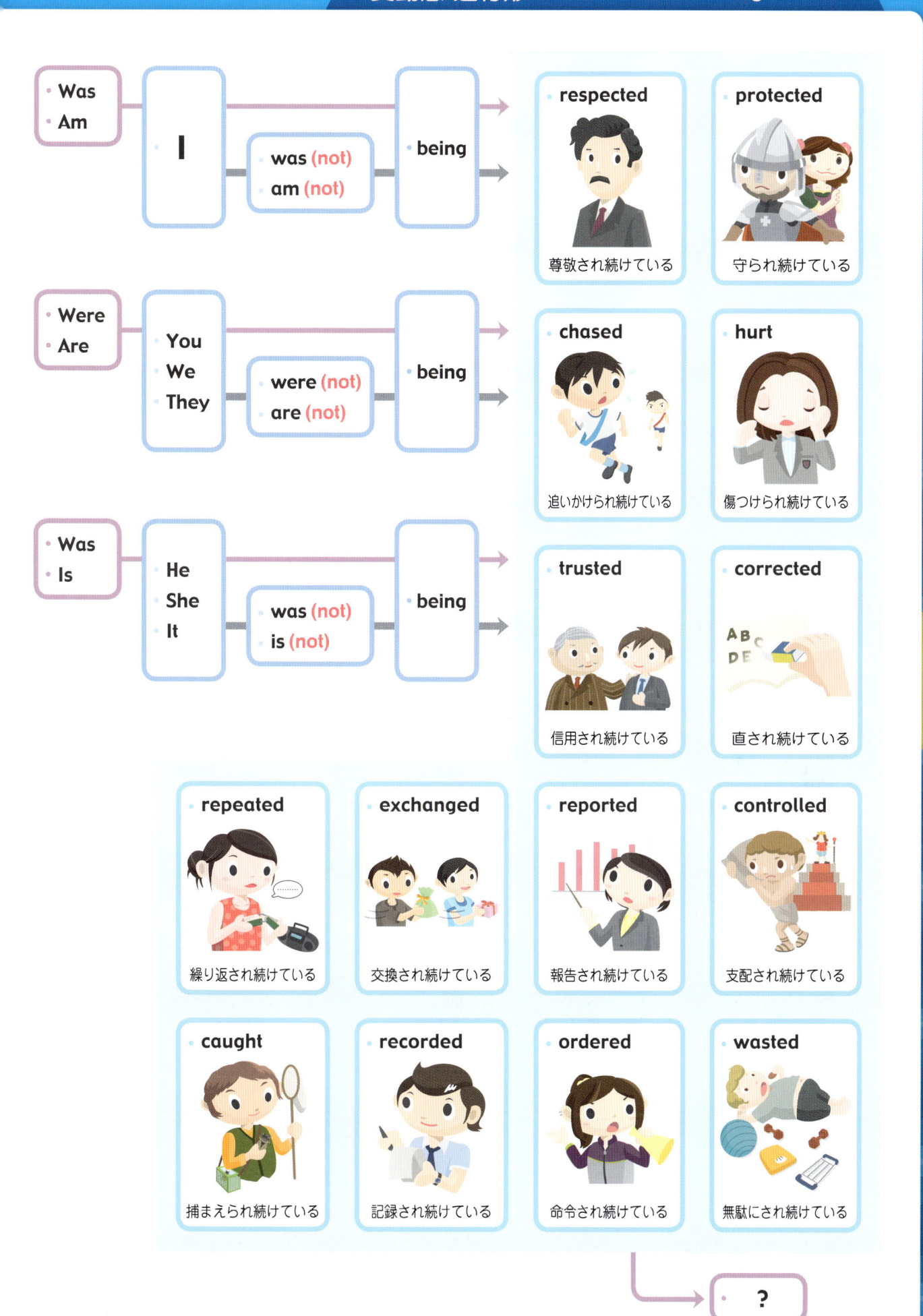

## 受動態 進行形　主語 + be動詞 + being + done

- Was
- Am

- I

- was (not)
- am (not)

- being

- **respected** 尊敬され続けている
- **protected** 守られ続けている

- Were
- Are

- You
- We
- They

- were (not)
- are (not)

- being

- **chased** 追いかけられ続けている
- **hurt** 傷つけられ続けている

- Was
- Is

- He
- She
- It

- was (not)
- is (not)

- being

- **trusted** 信用され続けている
- **corrected** 直され続けている

- **repeated** 繰り返され続けている
- **exchanged** 交換され続けている
- **reported** 報告され続けている
- **controlled** 支配され続けている
- **caught** 捕まえられ続けている
- **recorded** 記録され続けている
- **ordered** 命令され続けている
- **wasted** 無駄にされ続けている

- ?

Part 5

## Passive Continuous

### Practice / 練習

● P.50〜51 の時制チャートを参考に、自分で文章を作成してみよう。

**現在形**

I am being _____.

I am not being _____.

**過去形**

I was being _____.

I was not being _____.

**疑問形**

Are you being _____?

Were you being _____?

## 受動態 進行形　主語＋be動詞＋being＋done

# Practice Test / 確認テスト

| ！動詞ヒント | ・chase 追いかける | ・support 支える | ・protect 守る |
|---|---|---|---|
| | ・waste 無駄にする | ・trust 信用する | ・teach 教える |

① 次の文を肯定から否定にしてみよう。　　　　　　　　　　　　　　　　　　　　　※解答は P.57

例) I **am being controlled** by my family.　☞　I **am not being controlled** by my family.
　　　支配され続けている　　　家族から

1. A cat is being chased by a dog.　☞　A cat _____ by a dog.

2. The insects are being caught by the children.

　　☞ _____

② 次の文を肯定から疑問にしてみよう。

例) The father is being told about his daughter's studies by the teacher.
　　お父さん　言われ続けている　　　娘の勉強について　　　　先生から

　☞ Is the father being told about his daughter's studies by the teacher?

1. It is being protected.　☞　_____ it being protected?

2. The water is being wasted by you.

　　☞ _____

③ 次の文を現在形から過去形にしてみよう。

例) I **am being ordered** around by my mother.　☞　I **was being ordered** around by my mother.
　　　命令され続けている

1. He is being trusted by his teacher.　☞　He _____ by his teacher.

2. They are being taught mathematics.
　　　　　　　　　　　　　　算数

　　☞ _____

Part 5

## Passive Continuous

### Diary / えいご日記

**Pass The Exam!**
テストに合格する！

● 下線部に適切な語句を記入して、えいご日記を完成させよう。　　※解答は P.57

I am going to have an exam <u>next week</u>.
　　　　　　　　　　　　　　　　来　週

I am _____ by my teacher to study hard.
　　　　言われ続けている　　　　　　先生から　　　　　　一生懸命勉強する

After dinner, I was _____ _____
　　夕食後　　　　　　　　　教えられ続けている　　　　　　　　　　算　数

by my mother until 11 at <u>night</u>.
　　　　　　　　　　　　　　　　夜

I will <u>try my best</u> to pass the exam and <u>make my mother happy</u>!
　　　　がんばる　　　　　　　　　　　　　　　　　　お母さんを喜ばせる

!ヒント　　・tell 言う　　・teach 教える

● 上の文章を絵に描いてみよう。

受動態 進行形　主語 + be動詞 + being + done

● 左ページの日記を書き写そう。

## Question

● 質問に答えよう。その答えを下に書き写そう。

1. What are you going to have next week?

　☞　I am going to have _____ .

2. Were you being taught mathematics from after dinner until 11 at night?

　☞　Yes, I was. / No, I was not.

Part 5

## Passive Continuous

● 文章を自分で作ってみよう。

# 解 答 1

## Part 1：be 動詞 Be Verb

**Practice Test** 確認テスト（P.15）

① 1. *was*
   2. *You were young.*
   3. *He was from Tokyo.*

③ 1. *are not*
   2. *She is not my older sister.*
   3. *I am not young.*

② 1. *am going to be*
   2. *They are going to be 12 years old.*
   3. *She is going to be my friend.*

## Part 2：一般動詞 Simple Verb

**Practice Test** 確認テスト（P.29）

① 1. *stayed*
   2. *He flew back to Tokyo.*

③ 1. *Do*
   2. *Does she like fruit?*

② 1. *will meet*
   2. *He will wash his hands.*

**Diary** えいご日記（P.30） *made /_____（数字）/ played / threw / ate*

**Question**（P.31） 1. *I*　　2. *I / I*　　3. *I / I*

## Part 3：進行形 Continuous

**Practice Test** 確認テスト（P.37）

① 1. *am watching*
   2. *You are cooking my dinner.*

③ 1. *Are / studying*
   2. *Are they living in London?*

② 1. *are not feeding*
   2. *He is not drawing a picture.*

**Diary** えいご日記（P.38） *Today / eating / writing / hanging / swimming / like / like*

**Question**（P.39） 1. *Boy's Festival*　　2. *My father*
　　　　　　　　3. *eating / writing*

## Part 4：受動態 Passive

**Practice Test** 確認テスト（P.45）

① 1. *is shown*
   2. *I am introduced to her father by her.*

③ 1. *was told*
   2. *The horse was ridden by me.*

② 1. *are not given*
   2. *It is not made in India.*

**Diary** えいご日記（P.46） *is called / rainy season / Frogs / snails / are caught / Hydrangeas / are taken*

**Question**（P.47） 1. *rainy season*　　2. *Yes, there is.*
　　　　　　　　3. *frogs / snails / hydrangeas*

## Part 5：受動態 進行形 Passive Continuous

**Practice Test** 確認テスト（P.53）

① 1. *is not being chased*
   2. *The insects are not being caught by the children.*

③ 1. *was being trusted*
   2. *They were being taught mathematics.*

② 1. *Is*
   2. *Is the water being wasted by you?*

**Diary** えいご日記（P.54） *being told / being taught / mathematics*

**Question**（P.55） 1. *an exam*　　2. *Yes, I was.*

## 時制の一覧表　2

| | **Past**<br>ある時期からある時期まで | **Present**<br>今まで（に） | **Future**<br>未来のある時期 |
|---|---|---|---|
| **part 6**<br>完了形<br>Perfect<br>p.59 | had + done<br><br>もう〜してしまっていた<br>〜したことがあった<br>ずっと〜していた | ・has<br>・have + done<br><br>もう〜してしまっている（完了）<br>〜したことがある（経験）<br>ずっと〜している（継続） | ・will<br>・shall + have + done<br><br>〜しているでしょう |
| **part 7**<br>完了形<br>進行形<br>Perfect<br>Continuous<br>p.67 | had + been<br>+ do + ing<br><br>〜し続けていた | ・has<br>・have + been + do + ing<br><br>〜していた | ・will<br>・shall + have + been + do + ing<br><br>〜し続けているでしょう |
| **part 8**<br>完了形<br>受動態<br>Perfect<br>Passive<br>p.75 | had + been + done<br><br>〜されていた | ・has<br>・have + been + done<br><br>〜された | ・will<br>・shall + have + been + done<br><br>〜されているでしょう |
| 完了形<br>受動態<br>進行形<br>Perfect<br>Passive<br>Continuous | had + been<br>+ being + done<br><br>〜され続けていた | ・has<br>・have + been + being + done<br><br>〜され続けた | ・will<br>・shall + have + been + being + done<br><br>〜され続けているでしょう |

※文法上は可能だが、実生活においてはあまり使用されない。

# Part 6

# 完了形
## Perfect

主語（私は・あなたは…など）が
過去から現在までの時間の継続にまたがり
「もう〜した / してしまっている：完了」
「〜したことがある：経験」
「ずっと〜している：状態や動作の継続」
を表現したい時に使う文法です。

## Perfect

# 完了形　　主語 + have / has + done

|  | **Past** 過去のある時点まで（その時まで） | **Present** 過去から現在まで（今まで） | **Future** 未来のある時点ではそうなっていた（その時には） |
|---|---|---|---|
| ⭕ **Positive** 肯定 | • I had<br>• You / We / They had<br>• He / She / It had<br>　• done<br><br>・もう～してしまっていた<br>・～したことがあった<br>・ずっと～していた | • I have<br>• You / We / They have<br>• He / She / It has<br>　• done<br><br>・もう～してしまっている（完了）<br>・～したことがある（経験）<br>・ずっと～している（状態・動作が継続している） | • I / We — • will have done / • shall have done<br>• You / They / He / She / It<br>　• will have done<br><br>～しているでしょう |
| ❌ **Negative** 否定 | • I had<br>• You / We / They had<br>• He / She / It had<br>　• not done<br><br>・～したことがなかった<br>・～していなかった | • I have<br>• You / We / They have<br>• He / She / It has<br>　• not done<br><br>・～しなかった<br>・～したことがない<br>・ずっと～していない | • I / We — • will not have done / • shall not have done<br>• You / They / He / She / It<br>　• will not have done<br><br>～していないでしょう |
| ❓ **Question** 疑問 | • Had I<br>• Had you / we / they<br>• Had he / she / it<br>　• done …?<br><br>・～したことがありますか？<br>・～していましたか？ | • Have I<br>• Have you / we / they<br>• Has he / she / it<br>　• done …?<br><br>・～してしまいましたか？<br>・～したことがありますか？<br>・ずっと～していましたか？ | • Will / Shall — I / we<br>• Will — you / they / he / she / it<br>　• have done …?<br><br>～しているでしょうか？ |

過去から**過去のある時点**までに動作が完了し、その結果としての状態

過去から**現在**まで続いているその結果としての状態

**未来のある時点**である状態が続いた結果、状態がそうなった

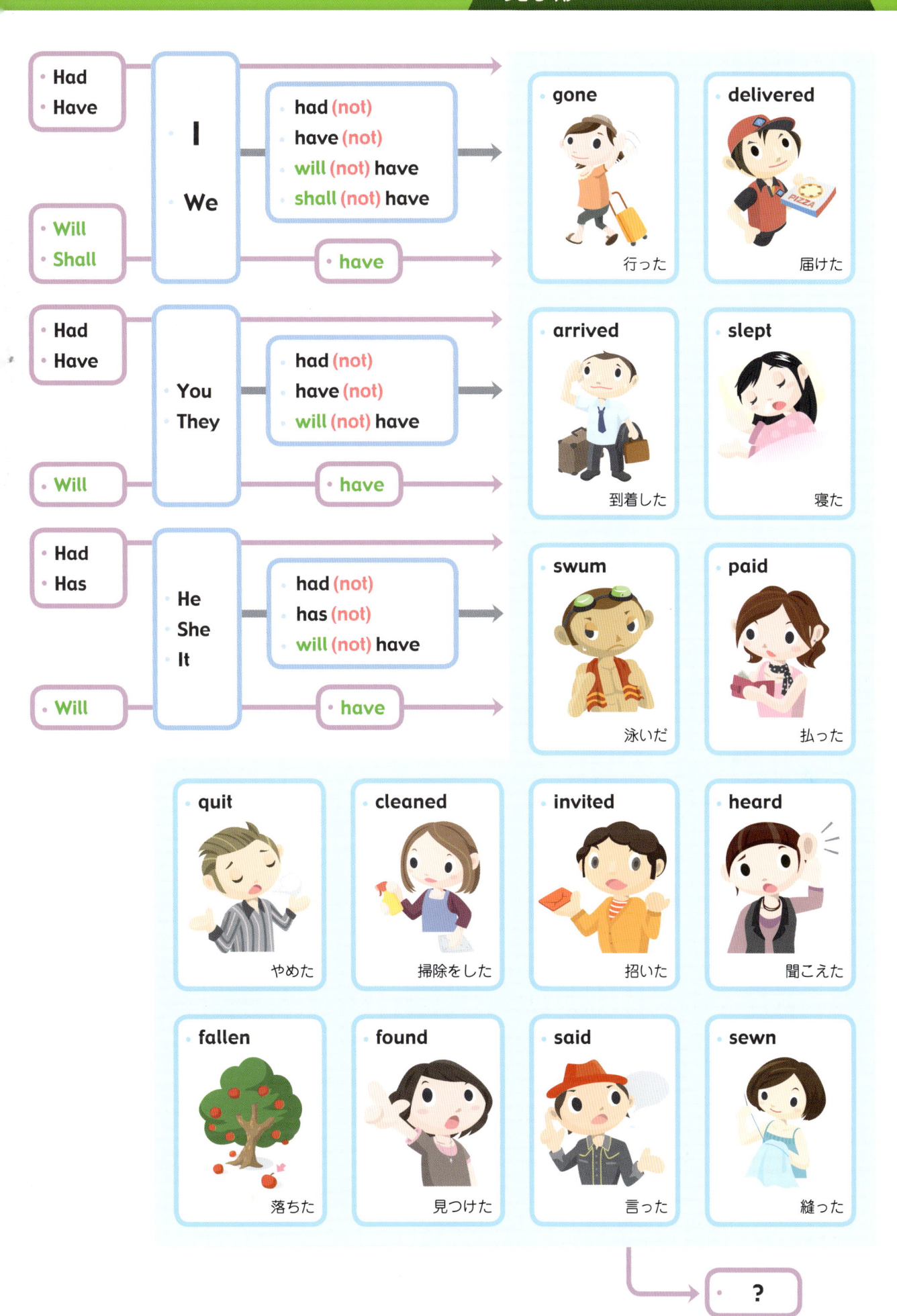

## 完了形　主語 + have / has + done

- Had
- Have

- Will
- Shall

I
We

- had (not)
- have (not)
- will (not) have
- shall (not) have

- have

- Had
- Have

- Will

You
They

- had (not)
- have (not)
- will (not) have

- have

- Had
- Has

- Will

He
She
It

- had (not)
- has (not)
- will (not) have

- have

- gone　行った
- delivered　届けた
- arrived　到着した
- slept　寝た
- swum　泳いだ
- paid　払った
- quit　やめた
- cleaned　掃除をした
- invited　招いた
- heard　聞こえた
- fallen　落ちた
- found　見つけた
- said　言った
- sewn　縫った
- ?

Part 6

sixty-one 61

## Perfect

### Practice / 練習

● P.60〜61を参考に、自分で文章を作成してみよう。

**現在形**

I have _____ .

I have not _____ .

**過去形**

I had _____ .

I had not _____ .

**未来形**

I will have _____ .

I will not have _____ .

**疑問形**

Have you _____ ?

Had you _____ ?

Will you have _____ ?

Part 6

## 完了形　主語 + have / has + done

## Practice Test / 確認テスト

!　動詞ヒント
- **stop** 止まる
- **give** 与える
- **clean** 掃除をする
- **quit** やめる
- **hear** 聞く

① 次の文を肯定から否定にしてみよう。　　　　　　　　　　　　　　※解答は P.91

例) Kanji <u>has eaten</u> lunch.　☞　Kanji has not eaten lunch.
　　　　　食べ終えた

1. The <u>rain</u> has stopped.
　　　　雨

　　☞　The rain _____.

2. She has given the <u>present</u> to her mother.
　　　　　　　　　　プレゼント

　　☞　_____

② 次の文を肯定から疑問にしてみよう。

例) She <u>has gone</u> to <u>Australia</u>.　☞　Has she gone to Australia?
　　　　行っている　　オーストラリアへ

1. He has cleaned his <u>room</u> <u>already</u>.
　　　　　　　　　　部屋　すでに

　　☞　_____ he _____ his room already?

2. They have quit studying <u>since graduating from school</u>.
　　　　　　　　　　　　　　学校を卒業して以来

　　☞　_____

3. You have already heard about <u>your new school</u>.
　　　　　　　　　　　　　　　新しい学校について

　　☞　_____

Part 6

## Perfect

### Diary / えいご日記　　Halloween ハロウィーン

● 下線部に適切な語句を記入して、えいご日記を完成させよう。

Tomorrow is Halloween.　　　　　　　　　　　　　　　　　　※解答は P.91

I _____ a costume for the party by last week.
　　作った　　　　　　衣装　　　　　　　パーティー　　先週までに

I had already finished my homework by yesterday.
　　　　終わった　　　　　宿題　　　　　昨日までに

I _____ some cookies for my friends by this morning.
　　焼いた　　　　クッキーをいくつか　　　　　　　　　今朝

I am ready for the _____.
　　用意できた　　　　　　パーティー

！ヒント　　• make 作る　　• bake 焼く

● 上の文章を絵に描いてみよう。

## 完了形　主語 + have / has + done

● 左ページの日記を書き写そう。

## Question

● 質問に答えよう。その答えを下に書き写そう。

1. What have you made for the party?

   ☞　I have made a _____ .

2. When did you finish your homework?

   ☞　I had finished my homework _____ .

Part 6

## Perfect

- 文章を自分で作ってみよう。

Part 6

# Part 7

## 完了形 進行形
### Perfect Continuous

主語（私は・あなたは… など）が
過去から現在までの時間の継続にまたがり
「〜していた」と表現する時に使う文法です。

## Perfect Continuous

# 完了形 進行形

主語 + have/has + been + doing

|  | **Past**<br>過去のある時点まで<br>（その時には） | **Present**<br>過去から現在まで継続して<br>（今まで） | **Future**<br>未来のある時点ではそう<br>なっていた（その時には） |
|---|---|---|---|
| **○ Positive 肯定** | • I<br>• You / We / They<br>• He / She / It<br>└ • had been doing<br>〜し続けていた | • I have<br>• You / We / They have<br>• He / She / It has<br>└ • been doing<br>〜していた | • I / We — • will have been doing / • shall have been doing<br>• You / They<br>• He / She / It<br>└ • will have been doing<br>〜し続けているでしょう |
| **× Negative 否定** | • I<br>• You / We / They<br>• He / She / It<br>└ • had not been doing<br>〜し続けていなかった | • I have<br>• You / We / They have<br>• He / She / It has<br>└ • not been doing<br>〜していなかった | • I / We — • will not have been doing / • shall not have been doing<br>• You / They<br>• He / She / It<br>└ • will not have been doing<br>〜し続けていないでしょう |
| **? Question 疑問** | • Had I<br>• Had you / we / they<br>• Had he / she / it<br>└ • been doing … ?<br>〜し続けていましたか？ | • Have I<br>• Have you / we / they<br>• Has he / she / it<br>└ • been doing … ?<br>〜していましたか？ | • Will/Shall I / we<br>└ • have been doing … ?<br>• Will<br>  ├ you / they<br>  │ └ • have been doing … ?<br>  └ he / she / it<br>    └ • have been doing … ?<br>〜し続けているでしょうか？ |

過去から**過去**のある時点までに
動作が完了し、その結果としての状態

過去から**現在**まで続いている
その結果としての状態

**未来**のある時点である状態が続いた
結果、状態がそうなった

Part 7

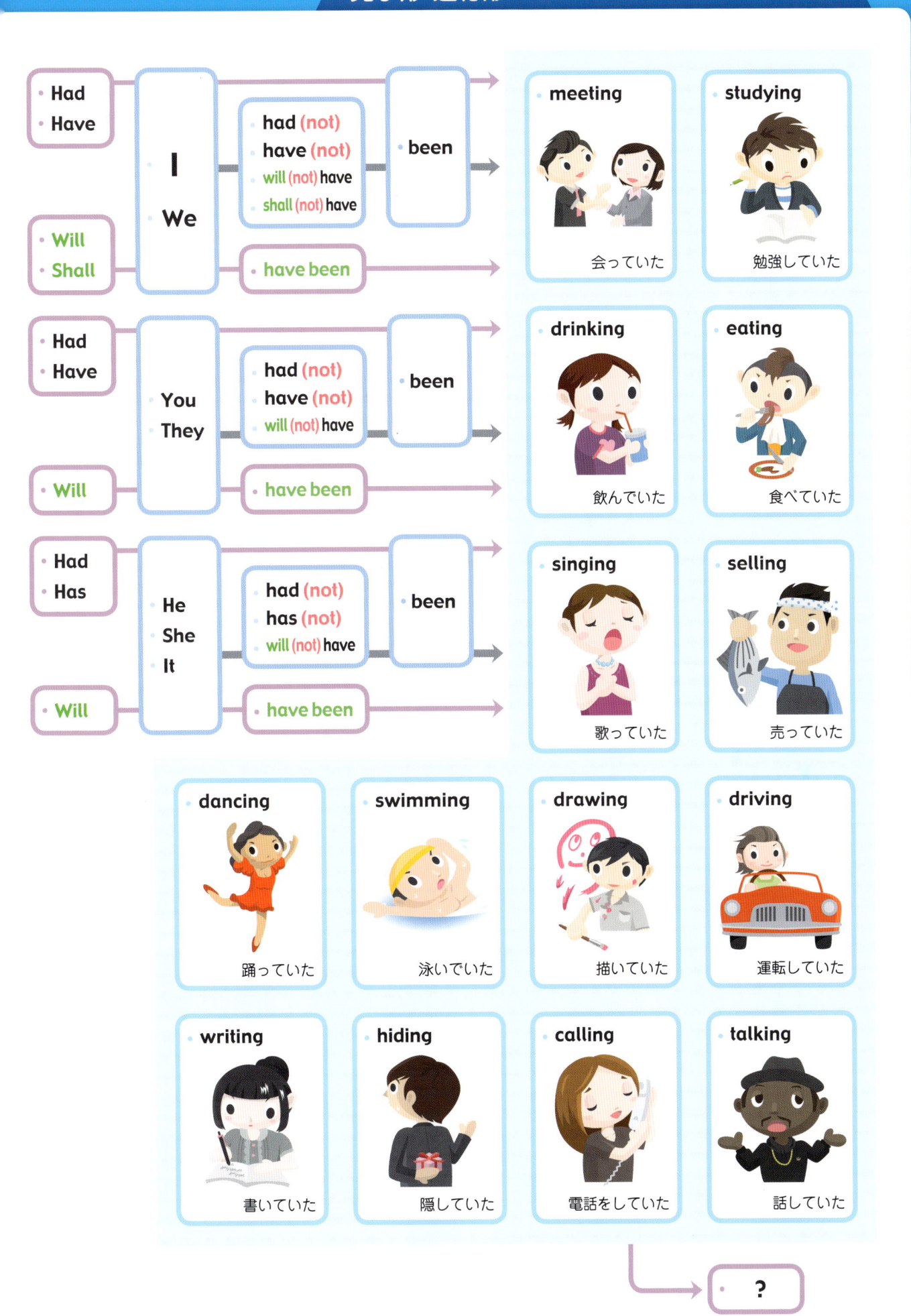

## 完了形 進行形　主語 + have/has + been + doing

- Had
- Have

- Will
- Shall

- I
- We

- had (not)
- have (not)
- will (not) have
- shall (not) have

- been
- have been

- Had
- Have

- Will

- You
- They

- had (not)
- have (not)
- will (not) have

- been
- have been

- Had
- Has

- Will

- He
- She
- It

- had (not)
- has (not)
- will (not) have

- been
- have been

- meeting 会っていた
- studying 勉強していた
- drinking 飲んでいた
- eating 食べていた
- singing 歌っていた
- selling 売っていた
- dancing 踊っていた
- swimming 泳いでいた
- drawing 描いていた
- driving 運転していた
- writing 書いていた
- hiding 隠していた
- calling 電話をしていた
- talking 話していた
- ?

sixty-nine 69

## Perfect Continuous

### Practice / 練習

● P.68〜69を参考に、自分で文章を作成してみよう。

**現在形**

I have been _____.

I have not been _____.

**過去形**

I had been _____.

I had not been _____.

**未来形**

I will have been _____.

I will not have been _____.

**疑問形**

Have you been _____?

Had you been _____?

Will you have been _____?

## 完了形 進行形　主語 + have/has + been + doing

## Practice Test / 確認テスト

| ！動詞ヒント | • drink 飲む | • sing 歌う | • dance 踊る |
|---|---|---|---|
| | • drive 運転する | • do する | |

① 次の文を肯定から否定にしてみよう。　　　　　　　　　　　　　　　　※解答は P.91

例) We have been eating cake since 3 o'clock.
　　　ずっと食べていた　　　　　　3時から
　☞ We have not been eating cake since 3 o'clock.

1. You have been drinking a glass of water for 10 minutes.
　　　　　　　　　　　　　　　　　水　　　　10分間の間
　☞ You _____ a glass of water for 10 minutes.

2. He has been singing songs during his break.
　　　　　　　　　　　　　　　　　　休憩の間
　☞ _____

② 次の文を肯定から疑問にしてみよう。

例) He has been drawing a picture all day. ☞ Has he been drawing a picture all day?
　　　ずっと絵を描いていた　　一日中

1. They have been dancing since last night.
　　　　　　　　　　　　　　昨晩から
　☞ _____ they been dancing since last night?

2. You have been driving for 5 hours.
　　　　　　　　　　　　　5時間の間
　☞ _____

3. He has been doing his homework until now.
　　　　　　　　　　　　　宿題
　☞ _____

Part 7

## Perfect Continuous

### Diary / えいご日記

**The Milky Way** 天の川

● 下線部に適切な語句を記入して、えいご日記を完成させよう。　※解答はP.91

The _____ is fine today.
　　　　天気　　　　晴れ

I saw a lot of stars in the _____.
　　　たくさんの星　　　　　　　　空

Beautiful stars that make up _____ come out at night.
　美しい　　　　　　作り上げる　　　　天の川　　　　　　　　　夜に出てくる

Yesterday, I wrote my wishes on some pieces of paper.
　　　　　　　　　　　願い事　　　　何枚か　　　　紙

I _____ to the stars for my wishes to come true.
　　ずっと祈り続けていた　　　　　星たちに　　　　願いがかなう

> ！ヒント　　・weather 天気　　・sky 空　　・pray 祈る

● 上の文章を絵に描いてみよう。

Part 7

## 完了形 進行形　主語 + have/has + been + doing

- 左ページの日記を書き写そう。

## Question

- 質問に答えよう。その答えを下に書き写そう。

1. *What did you write on the paper?*

   ☞　I wrote my _____ on the paper.


2. *Did you see a lot of stars in the sky?*

   ☞　Yes, I did. / No, I did not.

## Perfect Continuous

● 文章を自分で作ってみよう。

# Part 8

# 完了形 受動態
## Perfect Passive

主語（私は・あなたは… など）が
過去から現在までの時間の継続にまたがり
「〜された」と表現する時に使う文法です。

## Perfect Passive

# 完了形 受動態

**主語 + have/has + been + done**

|  | **Past**<br>過去のある時点まで<br>（その時には） | **Present**<br>過去から現在まで継続して<br>（今まで） | **Future**<br>未来のある時点ではそう<br>なっていた（その時には） |
|---|---|---|---|
| **○ Positive 肯定** | • I<br>• You / We / They<br>• He / She / It<br>└ • had been done<br>〜されていた | • I have<br>• You / We / They have<br>• He / She / It has<br>└ • been done<br>〜された | • I / We — • will have been done / • shall have been done<br>• You / They<br>• He / She / It<br>└ • will have been done<br>〜されているでしょう |
| **✕ Negative 否定** | • I<br>• You / We / They<br>• He / She / It<br>└ • had not been done<br>〜されていなかった | • I have<br>• You / We / They have<br>• He / She / It has<br>└ • not been done<br>〜されなかった | • I / We — • will not have been done / • shall not have been done<br>• You / They<br>• He / She / It<br>└ • will not have been done<br>〜されていないでしょう |
| **? Question 疑問** | • Had I<br>• Had you / we / they<br>• Had he / she / it<br>└ • been done … ?<br>〜されていましたか？ | • Have I<br>• Have you / we / they<br>• Has he / she / it<br>└ • been done … ?<br>〜されましたか？ | • Will/Shall — I / we<br>• Will — you / they / he / she / it<br>└ • have been done … ?<br>〜されているでしょうか？ |

過去から**過去**のある時点までに動作が完了し、その結果としての状態

過去から**現在**まで続いているその結果としての状態

**未来**のある時点である状態が続いた結果、状態がそうなった

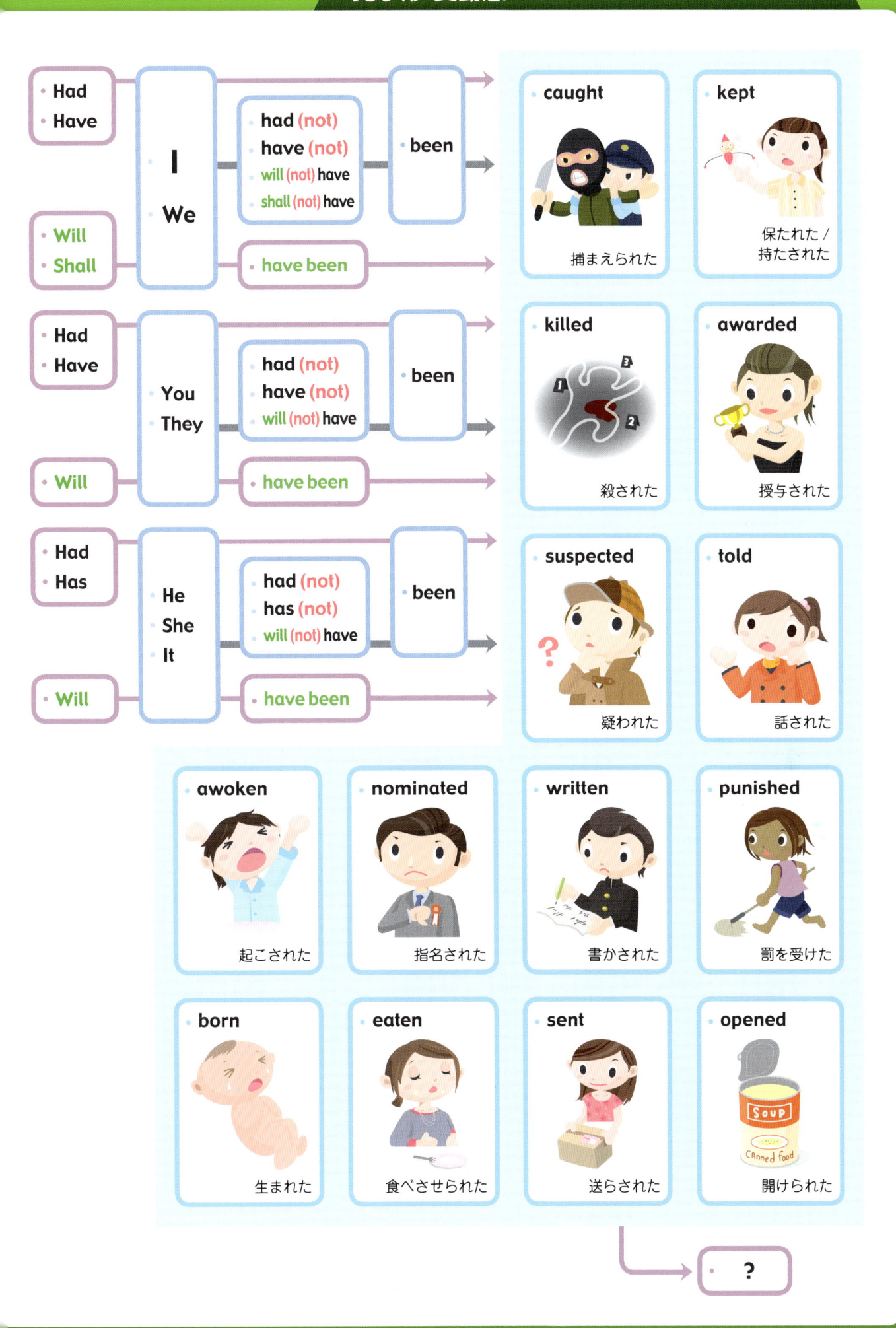

## 完了形 受動態　主語 + have/has + been + done

- Had
- Have

I / We
- had (not)
- have (not)
- will (not) have
- shall (not) have

been

- Will
- Shall

have been

- Had
- Have

You / They
- had (not)
- have (not)
- will (not) have

been

- Will

have been

- Had
- Has

He / She / It
- had (not)
- has (not)
- will (not) have

been

- Will

have been

- caught　捕まえられた
- kept　保たれた / 持たされた
- killed　殺された
- awarded　授与された
- suspected　疑われた
- told　話された
- awoken　起こされた
- nominated　指名された
- written　書かされた
- punished　罰を受けた
- born　生まれた
- eaten　食べさせられた
- sent　送らされた
- opened　開けられた
- ?

Part 8

seventy-seven　77

## Perfect Passive

### Practice / 練習

- P.76〜77を参考に、自分で文章を作成してみよう。

**現在形**

I have been _____.

I have not been _____.

**過去形**

I had been _____.

I had not been _____.

**未来形**

I will have been _____.

I will not have been _____.

**疑問形**

Have you been _____?

Had you been _____?

Will you have been _____?

## 完了形 受動態　主語 + have/has + been + done

### Practice Test / 確認テスト

> ! 動詞ヒント
> - wake up 起きる
> - tell 言う
> - keep 保つ / 続ける
> - nominate 指名する / ノミネートする

① 次の文を肯定から否定にしてみよう。　　　　　　　　　　　　※解答は P.91

例) The Christmas card has been sent already.
　　（クリスマスカード／送られた／すでに）

☞ The Christmas card has not been sent yet.
　　　　　　　　　　　　　　　　　　　　（まだ）

1. She has been woken up by her mother.

　☞ She _____ by her mother.

2. He has been told to finish his homework.
　　　　　　　　　　　　（終える）　（宿題）

　☞ _____

② 次の文を肯定から疑問にしてみよう。

例) You have been told to go to school.　☞　Have you been told to go to school?
　　　　　　　　　　　（学校へ行く）

1. The genie has been kept in a lamp since long ago.
　　　（魔人）　　　　　　　　　（ランプの中に）　（昔から）

　☞ _____ the genie been kept in a lamp since long ago?

2. He has been caught by the teacher already.
　　　　　　　　　　　　（先生に）

　☞ _____

3. You have been nominated for the prize.
　　　　　　　　　　　　　　　（賞に）

　☞ _____

Part 8

## Perfect Passive

### Diary / えいご日記　　　The Christmas Party / クリスマス会

● 下線部に適切な語句を記入して、えいご日記を完成させよう。　　※解答は P.91

Today I went to a _____ at my friend's house.
　　　　　　　　　　　クリスマス会　　　　　　　　　　　友達の家で

The invitation card _____ last month.
　　　招待状　　　　　すでに送られていた　　　　　先　月

I was invited !
　　招待された

From that day, I had been thinking about what to bring for a present...
　　　　　　　　　　考えていた　　　　　　　何を持っていくか　　プレゼントに

My friend gave me a pretty _____, and I gave her a beautiful _____.
　　　　　与えた　　　かわいい　　人形　　　　　　　　　　　きれいな　　　ドレス

We _____ the _____.
　　　楽しんだ　　　　　　クリスマス会

> ！ヒント　• send 送る　• doll 人形　• dress ドレス　• enjoy 楽しい

● 上の文章を絵に描いてみよう。

Part 8

## 完了形 受動態　主語 + have/has + been + done

- 左ページの日記を書き写そう。

## Question

- 質問に答えよう。その答えを下に書き写そう。

1. What did you give to your friend?

    ☞　I gave her a beautiful _____ .

2. Where did you have the Christmas party?

    ☞　The party was at my _____ .

## Perfect Passive

- 文章を自分で作ってみよう。

Part 9

# Can
重要な助動詞

主語が「〜できる」と表現する時に使います。

# ● Can

主語 ＋ can ＋ 動詞

※ will ＋ can の時は、"will be able to" に変化する。
※ can と not の間には、スペースを空けないのが一般的。

|  | Past 過去 | Present 現在 | Future 未来 |
|---|---|---|---|
| ○ Positive 肯定 | I / You / We / They / He / She / It → **could do** 〜できた | I / You / We / They / He / She / It → **can do** 〜できる | I / You / We / They / He / She / It → **will be able to do** 〜できるでしょう |
| × Negative 否定 | I / You / We / They / He / She / It → **could not do** 〜できなかった | I / You / We / They / He / She / It → **cannot do** 〜できない | I / You / We / They / He / She / It → **will not be able to do** 〜できないでしょう |
| ? Question 疑問 | **Could** I / you / we / they / he / she / it → **do ... ?** 〜できましたか？ | **Can** I / you / we / they / he / she / it → **do ... ?** 〜できますか？ | **Will** I / you / we / they / he / she / it → **be able to do ... ?** 〜できるでしょうか？ |

過去　現在　未来

Part 9

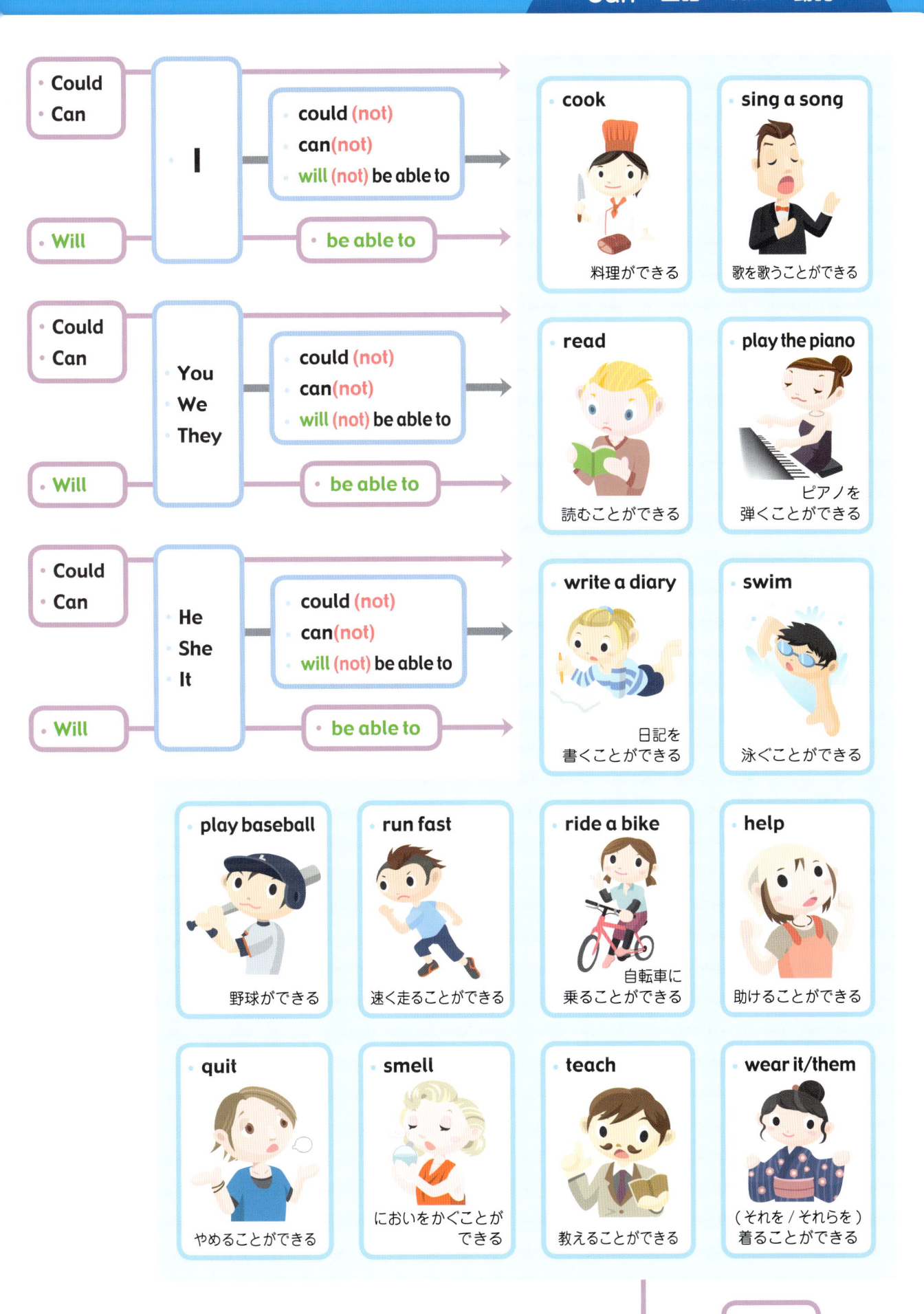

## Can  主語 + can + 動詞

- Could
- Can

- I
  - could (not)
  - can (not)
  - will (not) be able to

- Will → be able to

- Could
- Can

- You
- We
- They
  - could (not)
  - can (not)
  - will (not) be able to

- Will → be able to

- Could
- Can

- He
- She
- It
  - could (not)
  - can (not)
  - will (not) be able to

- Will → be able to

- cook — 料理ができる
- sing a song — 歌を歌うことができる
- read — 読むことができる
- play the piano — ピアノを弾くことができる
- write a diary — 日記を書くことができる
- swim — 泳ぐことができる
- play baseball — 野球ができる
- run fast — 速く走ることができる
- ride a bike — 自転車に乗ることができる
- help — 助けることができる
- quit — やめることができる
- smell — においをかぐことができる
- teach — 教えることができる
- wear it/them — （それを / それらを）着ることができる
- ?

Part 9

eighty-five 85

## Can

### Practice / 練習

● P.84～85 を参考に、自分で文章を作成してみよう。

**現在形**

I can _____ .

I cannot _____ .

**過去形**

I could _____ .

I could not _____ .

**未来形**

I will be able to _____ .

I will not be able to _____ .

**疑問形**

Can you _____ ?

Could you _____ ?

Will you be able to _____ ?

## Can　主語 + can + 動詞

## Practice Test / 確認テスト

| ！動詞ヒント | • swim 泳ぐ | • play 弾く | • drive 運転する |
| | • run 走る | • sleep 寝る | • dance 踊る |

① 次の文を肯定から否定にしてみよう。　　　　　　　　　　　　　　　　※解答は P.91

例) I <u>can write</u> a diary. ☞ I <u>cannot write</u> a diary.
　　　　書ける

1. He can swim. ☞ He _____ swim.

2. She can play the piano. ☞ _____

② 次の文を肯定から疑問にしてみよう。

例) You <u>can cook</u> <u>Japanese food</u>. ☞ Can you cook Japanese food?
　　　　料理ができる　　和食

1. She can drive a car. ☞ _____ she drive a car?

2. They can run fast. ☞ _____
　　　　　　　　速く

③ 次の文を現在形から過去形にしてみよう。

例) You <u>can help</u> your friend. ☞ You could help your friend.
　　　　助けることができる

1. He can sleep well. ☞ He _____ well.
　　　　　　　よく

2. They can dance very well. ☞ _____
　　　　　　　　　　とても上手に

Part 9

## Can

### Diary / えいご日記　　The Snowball Fight　雪合戦

● 下線部に適切な語句を記入して、えいご日記を完成させよう。　　※解答は P.91

The weather was snowy today.

My friends and I enjoyed a _____.
　友達と私は　　　楽しんだ　　　　　　　　雪合戦

I _____ my _____ with 3 snowballs.
　　当てることができた　　　　　　　　友　達

But my friends could not hit me with any _____.
　　　　　　　　　　　　　　　　　　　　　　　　　雪の玉

I won the game. I am so happy!
　勝った

!ヒント　・hit 当てる

● 上の文章を絵に描いてみよう。

Part 9

## Can 主語 ＋ can ＋ 動詞

● 左ページの日記を書き写そう。

## Question

● 質問に答えよう。その答えを下に書き写そう。

1. What did you enjoy today?

   ☞　I enjoyed the _____ .

2. How many snowballs did you hit your friends with?

   ☞　I hit my friends with _____ snowballs.

Part 9

## Can

- 文章を自分で作ってみよう。

# 解 答 2

## Part 6：完了形 Perfect

**Practice Test** 確認テスト（P.63）

① 1. has not stopped
   2. She has not given the present to her mother.
② 1. Has / cleaned
   2. Have they quit studying since graduating from school?
   3. Have you already heard about your new school?

**Diary** えいご日記（P.64） had made / had baked / party

**Question**（P.65） 1. costume
   2. by yesterday

## Part 7：完了形 進行形 Perfect Continuous

**Practice Test** 確認テスト（P.71）

① 1. have not been drinking
   2. He has not been singing songs during his break.
② 1. Have
   2. Have you been driving for 5 hours?
   3. Has he been doing his homework until now?

**Diary** えいご日記（P.72） weather / sky / The Milky Way / have been praying

**Question**（P.73） 1. wishes
   2. Yes, I did.

## Part 8：完了形 受動態 Perfect Passive

**Practice Test** 確認テスト（P.79）

① 1. has not been woken up
   2. He has not been told to finish his homework.
② 1. Has
   2. Has he been caught by the teacher already?
   3. Have you been nominated for the prize?

**Diary** えいご日記（P.80） Christmas party / had been sent / doll / dress / enjoyed / Christmas party

**Question**（P.81） 1. dress
   2. friend's house

## Part 9：Can（重要な助動詞）

**Practice Test** 確認テスト（P.87）

① 1. cannot
   2. She cannot play the piano.
② 1. Can
   2. Can they run fast?
③ 1. could sleep
   2. They could dance very well.

**Diary** えいご日記（P.88） snowball fight / could hit / friends / snowballs

**Question**（P.89） 1. snowball fight.
   2. 3

# 動詞変化表

動詞・名詞の語尾変化をマスターすると、いろいろな文章が書けるよ。

| 語尾の変化 | 動詞 (verb) | 名詞 (noun) |
|---|---|---|
| **基本形 ①** | 主語が He/She/It の時は動詞の語尾に s を付ける<br>think → thinks<br>live → lives | 名詞が2個以上の時は名詞の語尾に s を付ける<br>bird → birds<br>hotel → hotels |
| 動詞・名詞の語尾が<br>~o / ~s / ~sh / ~ch / ~x で終わる時 → **es** を付ける | fix → fixes<br>watch → watches<br>finish → finishes<br>go → goes<br>do → does | bus → buses<br>hairbrush → hairbrushes<br>box → boxes<br>sandwich → sandwiches |
| 動詞・名詞の語尾が<br>~y で終わる時 → **y→ies** にする | fly → flies<br>cry → cries<br>study → studies<br>try → tries | city → cities<br>baby → babies<br>sky → skies |
| 名詞の語尾が<br>~f / ~fe で終わる時 → **ves** にする | | shelf → shelves<br>knife → knives<br>elf → elves<br>wife → wives |
| **基本形 ②** | 動詞を過去形/過去分詞形に変化させる時は動詞の語尾に "ed" を付ける<br>ask → asked<br>wash → washed | |
| 動詞の語尾が<br>~y で終わる時 → **y→ied** にする | study → studied<br>try → tried<br>marry → married | |
| 動詞・名詞の語尾が<br>~ay / ~ey / ~oy / ~uy で終わる時 → 基本形と同じ | play → played<br>enjoy → enjoyed<br>stay → stayed<br>例外 say → said / pay → paid など | key → keys<br>boy → boys<br>toy → toys<br>way → ways |
| **基本形 ③** | 動詞を進行形に変化させる時は動詞の語尾に "ing" を付ける<br>watch → watching<br>cook → cooking | |
| 動詞の語尾が<br>~e で終わる時 → **e** を取る | make → making<br>write → writing | |
| 動詞の語尾が<br>~ie で終わる時 → **ie→y** にする | lie → lying<br>tie → tying | |

## ふろく　動詞変化表 verb noun

| 母音 vowel | : a e i o u |
|---|---|
| 子音 consonant | : b c d f g h j k l m n p q r s t v w x y z |

**~ing / ~ed** を単語の語尾に付ける時

① 単語の最後のアルファベットを繰り返す場合

| 単語の語尾 | 動詞 (verb) |
|---|---|
| vowel（母音）<br>~a<br>~e<br>~i<br>~o<br>~u<br>**+** consonant（子音）<br>語尾が「母音＋子音」の時 | stop → stopped<br>　　　　 stopping<br>run → running<br>最後のアルファベットを2回繰り返す |

② 単語の最後のアルファベットを繰り返さない場合

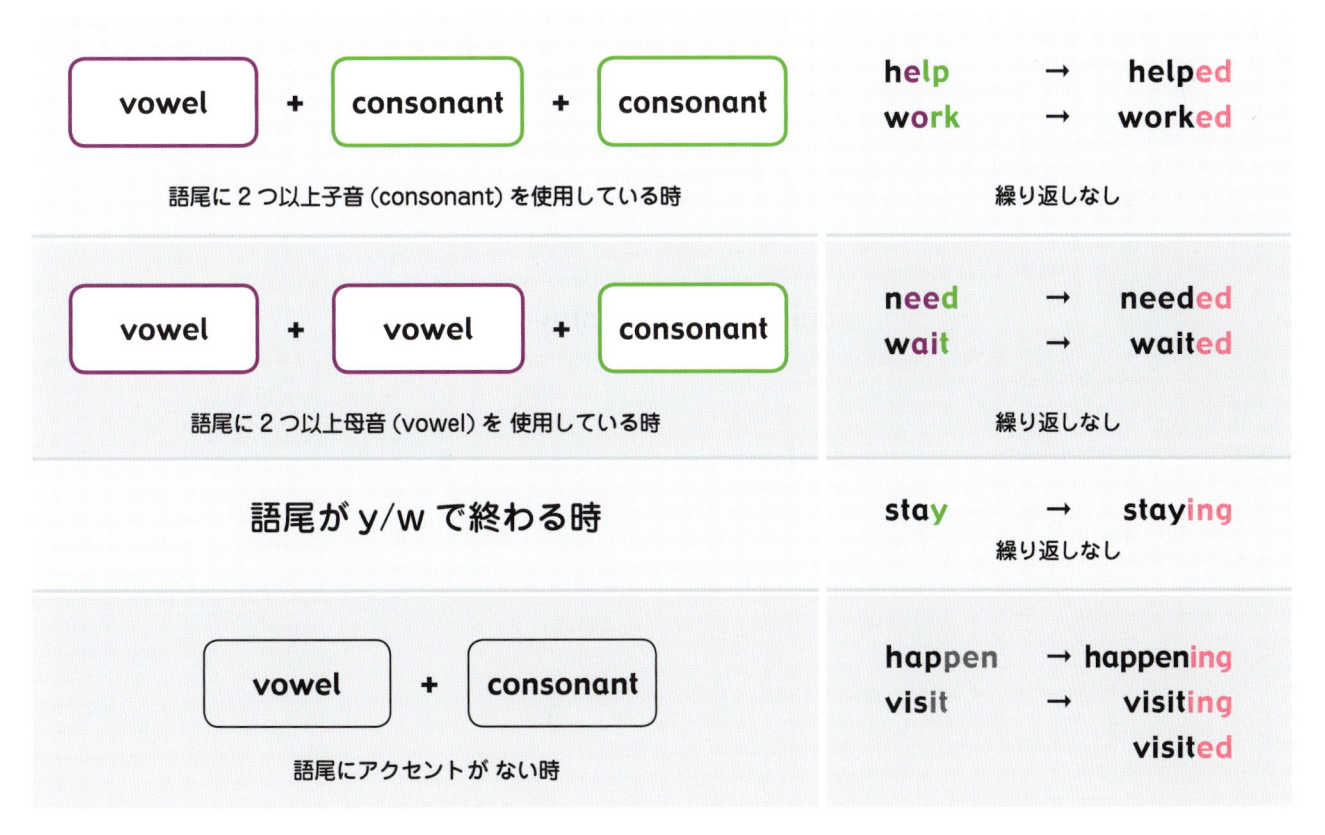

| | |
|---|---|
| vowel + consonant + consonant<br>語尾に2つ以上子音 (consonant) を使用している時 | help → helped<br>work → worked<br>繰り返しなし |
| vowel + vowel + consonant<br>語尾に2つ以上母音 (vowel) を使用している時 | need → needed<br>wait → waited<br>繰り返しなし |
| 語尾が y/w で終わる時 | stay → staying<br>繰り返しなし |
| vowel + consonant<br>語尾にアクセントが ない時 | happen → happening<br>visit → visiting<br>　　　　 visited |

※これらのルールに沿わないものもあります。

## 不規則動詞の変化表

| 日本語 Japanese | 原型 infinitive (do) | 過去型 past simple (did) | 過去分詞 past participle (done) |
|---|---|---|---|
| ある | is / am / are (be) | was / were | been |
| 起こす | awake | awoke | awoken |
| 打つ | beat | beat | beaten |
| （〜に）なる | become | became | become |
| 始める | begin | began | begun |
| 曲げる | bend | bent | bent |
| かむ | bite | bit | bitten |
| 吹く | blow | blew | blown |
| 壊す | break | broke | broken |
| 持ってくる | bring | brought | brought |
| 建てる | build | built | built |
| 買う | buy | bought | bought |
| 捕まえる | catch | caught | caught |
| 選ぶ | choose | chose | chosen |
| 来る | come | came | come |
| （お金）かかる | cost | cost | cost |
| 切る | cut | cut | cut |
| 死ぬ | die | died | died |
| （〜を）する | do | did | done |
| 引く | draw | drew | drawn |
| 飲む | drink | drank | drunk |
| （車を）運転する | drive | drove | driven |
| 食べる | eat | ate | eaten |
| 落ちる | fall | fell | fallen |
| 感じる | feel | felt | felt |
| 戦う | fight | fought | fought |
| 見つける | find | found | found |
| 飛ぶ | fly | flew | flown |
| 忘れる | forget | forgot | forgotten |
| 得る | get | got | gotten |
| 与える | give | gave | given |
| 行く | go | went | gone |
| 成長する | grow | grew | grown |
| かける / つり下げる | hang | hung | hung |
| 持つ | have | had | had |
| 聞く | hear | heard | heard |
| 隠す | hide | hid | hidden |
| 打つ | hit | hit | hit |
| 保つ / 持ちこたえる | hold | held | held |
| 傷つける | hurt | hurt | hurt |
| 保つ / 続ける | keep | kept | kept |
| 知る | know | knew | known |
| 去る | leave | left | left |

## ふろく 不規則動詞の変化表 verb noun

| 日本語 Japanese | 原型 infinitive (do) | 過去型 past simple (did) | 過去分詞 past participle (done) |
| --- | --- | --- | --- |
| 貸す | lend | lent | lent |
| させる | let | let | let |
| 横たわる | lie | lay | lain |
| 失う | lose | lost | lost |
| 作る | make | made | made |
| 会う | meet | met | met |
| まちがえる | mistake | mistook | mistaken |
| 払う | pay | paid | paid |
| 置く | put | put | put |
| やめる | quit | quit | quit |
| 読む | read | read | read |
| 乗る | ride | rode | ridden |
| のぼる | rise | rose | risen |
| 走る | run | ran | run |
| 言う | say | said | said |
| 見る | see | saw | seen |
| 売る | sell | sold | sold |
| 送る | send | sent | sent |
| 縫う | sew | sewed | sewn |
| 振る | shake | shook | shaken |
| 光る | shine | shone | shone |
| 見せる | show | showed | shown |
| 閉じる | shut | shut | shut |
| 歌う | sing | sang | sung |
| 座る | sit | sat | sat |
| 眠る | sleep | slept | slept |
| 話す | speak | spoke | spoken |
| 費やす | spend | spent | spent |
| 広げる | spread | spread | spread |
| はねる | spring | sprang | sprung |
| 立つ | stand | stood | stood |
| 盗む | steal | stole | stolen |
| 突き刺す | stick | stuck | stuck |
| ふくらむ | swell | swelled | swollen |
| 泳ぐ | swim | swam | swum |
| 取る | take | took | taken |
| 教える | teach | taught | taught |
| 話す | tell | told | told |
| 考える | think | thought | thought |
| 投げる | throw | threw | thrown |
| 結ぶ | tie | tied | tied |
| わかる | understand | understood | understood |
| 目が覚める | wake | woke | woken |
| 着ている | wear | wore | worn |
| 書く | write | wrote | written |

## Message

子どもたちが英語を、自然に身につけられるようにしたい。
それが諸外国への距離を縮め、世界基準でものを考えることにつながり、ひいては、地球規模の視野を獲得してくれると確信して、子どもたちへのレッスンを続けてきました。
その中から「難しい文法用語や日本語での説明をせず、英文法を視覚でイメージ理解させるのが効果的」との信念を得て、試行錯誤の末、本書の「時制チャート」「日記シート」を完成させることができました。
この本を作り上げるまでに、多くの方々のサポートや励ましに支えられてきました。感謝の気持ちでいっぱいです。

三修社の松居奈都さんは、いつも私の出す原稿をスマートに編集してくれました。
ラブデザインの越阪部ワタルさんは、前作でも大好評だったイラストはもちろん、今回も素敵なデザインで、さらに「目で見て理解できる」本へと仕上げてくださいました（イラストの入った原稿を初めて見た時の感動は、今でも忘れられません）。ひとつひとつのイラストに込められたストーリーを子どもたちと想像しながら眺めていると、自然に笑みがこぼれます。ぜひ、みなさんも楽しんでください。
教室の講師 Mr. Craig Adlard, Ms. Rajni Verma, Mr. Timo Perttu は、原稿チェックやアドバイスなど惜しみなく協力してくれました。
教室の子どもたちや保護者の方々にも、多くのお力添えをいただきました（本書の仕上がりを楽しみにしている子どもたちの姿は、かわいくて仕方がありません）。
また、仕事に忙しい母を理解し励まし、一緒に喜んでくれる家族の存在があればこそ、頑張ることができました。

最後に、この本を手に取ってくださったみなさん、本当にありがとうございます。
この本によってお子さまたちが「英語ってかんた～ん！」と楽しく学んでくれることを願っています。そして、地球上の子どもたちがグローバルな心を育むことで将来、世界中の人々が幸せな世の中になるよう祈っています。

すべてに感謝の気持ちを込めて。

能島 久美江

---

### えいごで日記　文法　動詞・時制

2010年8月10日　第1刷発行
2021年8月10日　第5刷発行

著　者　　能島 久美江
発行者　　前田 俊秀
発行所　　株式会社 三修社
　　　　　〒150-0001　東京都渋谷区神宮前 2-2-22
　　　　　TEL 03-3405-4511　FAX 03-3405-4522
　　　　　振替 00190-9-72758
　　　　　https://www.sanshusha.co.jp
　　　　　編集担当　松居 奈都

ブックデザイン・イラスト　　越阪部 ワタル（ラブデザイン）

印刷・製本　　株式会社 リーブルテック

©Kumie Noujima 2010 Printed in Japan
ISBN978-4-384-05610-5　C8082

---

JCOPY〈出版者著作権管理機構 委託出版物〉
本書の無断複製は著作権法上での例外を除き禁じられています。複製される場合は、そのつど事前に、出版者著作権管理機構（電話 03-5244-5088 FAX 03-5244-5089 e-mail: info@jcopy.or.jp）の許諾を得てください。